P9-CQL-177

# Listening Ministry

"Susan Hedahl draws from foundational texts and theories on listening to inform the listening task, to which the church has been called. Her experience as one who listens regularly and faithfully in classroom and community brings rich insight into this fine work."

—Rev. Janyce C. Jorgensen
Lower Susquehanna Synod, ELCA

# *Listening Ministry*

## Rethinking Pastoral Leadership

Susan K. Hedahl

Fortress Press

Minneapolis

LISTENING MINISTRY
Rethinking Pastoral Leadership

Cover and book design: Zan Ceeley
Cover art: *Ecriteau* by Ed Paschke, courtesy of Ed Paschke/SuperStock, Inc.
    Used with permission.

Library of Congress Cataloging-in-Publication Data

Hedahl, Susan K. (Susan Karen)
    Listening ministry : rethinking pastoral leadership / Susan K. Hedahl.
        p. cm.
    Includes bibliographical references.
    ISBN 0-8006-3174-9 (alk. paper)
        1. Pastoral theology. 2. Christian leadership. 3. Listening—Religious
    aspects—Christianity. I. Title.

    BV4011.H364 2001
    253—dc21                                                    00-067692

Manufactured in the U.S.A.                                      AF 1–3174
06    05    04    03    02    01    1    2    3    4    5    6    7    8    9    10

*For three of God's superlative listeners*

*Carolyn Coakley Hickerson*

*Andrew Wolvin*

*Norma Schweitzer Wood*

# Contents

# Preface

Though unknown to me at the time, this book had its genesis in the summer of 1963. Like most Minnesotans of Scandinavian descent, the genetic propensity to "go to the summer cabin" was true for our family. That year our library book bag contained a novel by Taylor Caldwell entitled *The Listener*.[1]

In brief, the book begins with the description of a philanthropist's gift to a city park—a building with the words THE LISTENER chiseled over the entrance. The story relates the conflicted narratives of several people who share them with the unknown listener, whose identity is not divulged until the final chapter. The story haunts me even more today, with the additional templates of my nine years of work as a homiletics instructor and twenty-five years as a Lutheran pastor.

Like others in ministry, I number among my most significant moments those times when another human being and I listened to one another in a genuine, caring manner. I value those encounters in the larger context of so much presumed and ineffective listening that constitutes much of our communication efforts with one another. Likewise, I value the respectful, faithful hearings that others have given to me when I needed their receptive silence. These have greatly influenced my sense of how vital good listening is for effective pastoral leadership.

A number of people helped to create this book, and I am grateful to them for that. Some of these include participants of the spring 1997 Gettysburg Lutheran Theological Seminary course on listening: Eric Ash, Maureen Chandler, Janet Comings, Beth Folkemer, Glenn Foster, William Gies, Janyce and Richard Jorgensen, George Minick,

Karen Minnich-Sadler, Charles Peterson, Sylvia Rosemergy, Antony Sebastian, Joseph Skillman, Dona Van Ech, Robert Yankovitz. It was a mixed denominational group—Lutheran, Episcopalian, and Catholic. They opened up many new connections between listening and ministry for all of us.

I also note my gratitude here to co-teacher of that course and dean of the seminary, Norma Schweitzer Wood. Among her multiple talents is that of superlative and compassionate listening, as all who know her will testify.

Special thanks are due Andrew Wolvin and Carolyn Coakley Hickerson, coauthors of the primary research compendium on listening.[2] It is our seminary's good fortune to have Andy close by at the University of Maryland in the Department of Communication. For his commitment to listening, his Christian faith perspective, and his helpfulness with this book, enough cannot be said. His colleague and coauthor, Carolyn Coakley Hickerson, also shared some of her insights with us from California, as have a number of friends in the International Listening Association. Carolyn's life ended prematurely and tragically in 2000 because of cancer; much in this book stands as a living memorial to her pioneering work in the field of listening.

For the conversation community that is our seminary faculty— thank you. I can always count on the fact that you are ready to share one more book, one more quote, one more great idea. A number of people offered specific resources and advice about their vocational understandings of listening.

Thank you to Gilson Waldkoenig, associate professor of Church in Society, and Richard P. Carlson, associate professor of Biblical Studies, who are both members of our faculty; Paul Derrickson, director of Clinical Pastoral Education at Hershey Medical Center, Hershey, Pennsylvania; and Alan Wenrich, former assistant to the bishop in the Lower Susquehanna Synod of the Evangelical Lutheran Church in America.

There are other listeners in my life who have formed this book. You know who you are. My heartfelt thanks to each of you for teaching me that listening is an act of patient friendship, love, and the very imaging of a listening God in our relationships.

# Introduction

"Mary . . . sat at the Lord's feet and listened to what he was saying."
—LUKE 10:39

During the autumn of 1997, a group of ministers met in Carlisle, Pennsylvania, for a presentation and discussion about ministry and listening. One participant asked plaintively, "Who will teach us to listen for God—and to each other?" The silence that followed accurately reflects the current vacuum of listening education for those in pastoral leadership ministry.

*Listening Ministry* examines the role listening plays in the lives of those engaged in lay and ordained ministry and entertains several ambitious intentions. It intends to provide the first blueprint, sometimes experimental in nature, for a theology of listening. As such, it provides a theological rationale for the development of good listening skills emerging from the witness of scriptural, pastoral, and theological traditions. That this book developed out of the author's work and experiences as a homiletician and pastor might be considered ironic or in direct contradiction to the Protestant emphasis on word, speech, and proclamation. However, the activities of listening—its meanings, presuppositions, intentions, and effects—offer a needed reformation for both our ministry leadership and for the nature of our theological speech in a word-saturated world. Foreground and background are inseparable.

*Listening Ministry* describes the critical role of listening—the most basic field of speech communications—in all aspects of pastoral leadership and ministry. By doing so, it challenges the assumption that traditional listening patterns and skills are only the purview of good pastoral counseling methods. In fact, the act of listening extends into all arenas of ministry, with corresponding shifts in listening patterns, attitudes, and behaviors dependent on context.

We all speak frequently and in many ways. But who, after all is said and done, really listens? In fact, we rarely stop to consider the dynamics of listening. Yet listening is the primary trajectory of all other communication acts. It is the first learned type of communication, the most predominant of all speech communication acts, and often the last ability exercised before death.[1] Listening is a key component in the way individuals and organizations function with one another; it has a direct bearing on the ways power and authority are exercised. An inability or refusal to listen could result in death, both spiritual and physical. It is the life-giving connective link between God and humanity. Yet listening is a communication skill often ignored and little understood.

The evolution of this book started in the homiletics classrooms of Gettysburg Lutheran Theological Seminary. Like homiletics instructors in most faith perspectives, I spent my classroom time mainly listening to and commenting on student preaching. After awhile, however, it seemed insufficient to me to limit my remarks to delivery and sermon construction alone. Necessary questions related to inclusive language and theology fell short of some needed further step—but what? What did classroom preaching and commentary leave untouched? I was uncertain as to what was missing.

Through the Speech Communication Association and its multiple interest groups, I came across the International Listening Association.[2] Because of interaction with that group, I moved toward a pedagogical and personal approach that situates me primarily as a listener to proclamation, along with other listeners-in-community. That change in perspective radically changed my views of teaching, pastoral leadership, and ministry. The reader will see these ideas more fully explored in the coming pages.

In turn, the insights gained in the homiletics classrooms evolved into a course on listening for church leaders in the spring of 1997. I taught the classes with Norma Wood, a counselor by vocation and now dean of the seminary. We believe the course was the first of its kind in any venue of theological education. With no book available on listening ministry, we used the seminal work *Listening* by college professors

Andrew Wolvin and Carolyn Gwynn Coakley.[3] Their rich, in-depth research and the resultant taxonomy of listening levels are referred to frequently in these pages; they serve as the dialogue partner and theoretical spine of this volume. The reader is encouraged to pursue this primary source on listening.

Those pondering the thoughtful incorporation of better listening practices into their ministries will no doubt encounter what the class did in dialogue with listening theory. We were intrigued with what it meant to view ministry primarily as listener rather than as speaker and doer. We continually found ourselves caught off guard, our biases and methods of ministry challenged by what seemed obvious yet was often difficult to practice or even to understand. We found we actually knew very little about the processes involved in listening. We wondered constantly why our training had so completely ignored such a crucial human element of communication in the lives of faith communities. The almost offhanded nature of listening continually double backed on us with multiple surprises.

Early in the course it became apparent that the listening typology provided by the Wolvin-Coakley work demonstrated the total absence of any research or written materials specifically for pastoral leaders on listening. Of necessity, this book has become, in part, a "class act." It reflects and encompasses many of the issues, frustrations, and insights the students brought from their varied ministry sites. The pastoral listening venues identified in these pages reflect the participants' creativity and their plans to specify listening tactics as a consciously developed part of their ministries. They contributed to the three major, related definitions of pastoral listening introduced in chapter 1 and explored more fully throughout *Listening Ministry*.

Based on these struggles, this volume is an unabashed effort to start the conversation about making the connections among these three components: pastoral ministry, leadership, and listening skills. This is an invitation to look at pastoral leadership in a completely different way. In these pages the reader will find a blend of theological thinking on listening, new and tested research, suggested forms of listening education and skills assessment, and a continuing effort to understand listening as the heart of effective and faithful ministry.

The book encompasses several dynamics related to ministry and listening. First, it situates the listening event among leaders and those to whom they minister. This book cannot be regarded as solo continuing theological education; listening always involves "the other" or "others," making it an intensely community-based and context-centered activity. Learning listening skills can happen only when the learner practices, and faith communities are often eager to participate with leadership in this mutual means of deepening their lives and work.

Second, pastoral leadership listening is set within the context of its adjacent and interactive influences. These involve nonverbal behaviors such as silence and the variety of "contact codes'" related to the ordering of time, space, touch, and varieties of verbal expressiveness that form the act of listening.[4] Complicating and enriching the listening process are also the multiple factors of age, gender, race, personality, power, and context.

Finally, the types of listening referred to throughout address both individual and corporate forms of listening. The Wolvin-Coakley taxonomy, together with the pioneering work developed through the Gettysburg Seminary class discussions, will demonstrate the multilayered components of listening involved as the pastoral leader moves through a variety of listening venues—ranging from the individual to groups to the entire congregation, as well as to other communities outside the parish.

Listening is contextual. A college instructor intent on teaching listening competencies, or a pilot learning the life-and-death needs of listening well in the cockpit, enter the field with intentions and needs different from the professional pastoral leader. What follows in these pages will cover some of the basics involved in good listening regardless of the setting, but with a special eye to the needs of ministry.

Since the field of communications termed "listening" covers many areas, this work is primarily devoted to listening as a skill that intersects all areas of pastoral ministry. Specialized listening settings related to those who suffer hearing loss or impairment are exempted from this volume since the field of study in this area has its own rich and extensive literature. While acknowledging the contributions of other adjacent fields, this is not a book on listening based on pastoral counseling (with its attendant verbal frames and techniques), pastoral theology, psychology, the contemplative tradition, or parish management— helpful as those materials are. I refer to these contributory areas only with the intention of continuing the focus on listening skills as a bridge to all ministry settings.

In chapter 1, basic definitions, understandings, and benefits of listening are introduced. They describe listening generally, within the possibilities and constraints of pastoral listening. Successive chapters explore the settings and enactments of listening communication in its different pastoral forms. The reader will note that each chapter introduces a number of new ideas, some of which are explored fully with others offered in outline form only, as further prompts for the reader's own thinking and research. Every chapter concludes with questions for discussion that are useful in ministry settings of many types. The intent of the extensive bibliography at the book's conclusion is to further whet the appetite of the reader in developing her or his own theology of ministry that includes good listening.

However, perhaps the most significant struggle the pastoral leader will have is simply to consider how to listen better. Trained as fixers of humanity, the minister will find that the best response to the pastoral question "What can I *do?*" resides in the place of loving and gracious listening.

*One*

# Ministry and Listening Leadership: What Are the Foundations?

The more faithfully you listen to the voice within you, the better you will hear what is sounding outside you, and only the one who listens can speak. Is this the starting point of the road towards the union of your two dreams—to be allowed in clarity of mind to mirror life and in purity of heart to mold it?
                                                              —Dag Hammarskjöld, *Markings*

Retired Swedish film director Ingmar Bergman recently authored a work of fiction called *Private Confessions*. Set in Sweden in the 1920s, the novel's main character, Anna, is a pastor's wife whose confessions to a trusted uncle, her husband, and a woman friend provide a journal of her failing marriage, an affair, and her relationship with God. Uncle Jacob offers Anna a biblical summary of the dilemma her own confessions have produced for her as she confronts several decisions: "They [the disciples] have listened to the message of invincible love. The Master has looked at them and they have turned their faces toward him. They have listened and understood. They have realized they were chosen."[1]

## Listening and Ministry

All ministry genuinely committed to listening implies this divine-human relationship of responsive listening and the call to faith commitment. This is true for both the pastoral listener and the speaker, whose own faith commitments may be minimal. To listen well is to enact the path of commitment and to engage the speaker in the same. On the part of the minister, good pastoral listening is no less than an act of faith.

A unique aspect of ministry is that just about anybody for any reason might seek a pastoral listener. The open door of the pastoral minister represents a profound freedom that exists in no other place in society. One may hear virtually anything at any time from anybody in any condition of mind, soul, and physical health. The listening relationship can present an almost endless spectrum of needs, interests, motivations, pains, and challenges for both speaker and listener.

Knowing our own thirst for a good listener, is it possible that we have overlooked one of the most important areas of pastoral ministry in our training and thinking—listening? Listening is, I am convinced, a little-understood treasure awaiting discovery, professionally and personally. Moreover, it is not something new; it is a long-embedded part of almost all spiritual traditions.

For too long, however, ministry providers and educators have assumed that listening skills just happen—little thought is given to the need for knowledge or training in the field. The emphases in theological education of all types lends credence to this assumption. Descriptions of theological education are defined by the verbs that fill our seminary and theological school catalogues: *doing* ministry, *presiding* at Eucharist, *preaching* the Word, *facilitating* meetings, *engaging* in field work, *working* in rural areas. Additionally, words that cluster around listening—such as prayer, meditation, and spirituality—are often minimally listed or omitted. Nowhere is the word *listening* used, whether as the major emphasis of a course, in a mission statement, or heading the list of needed ministry skills.[2] Praxis rules the day—but what kind? In our efforts to survive and thrive theologically, are we drowning in our own verbiage because we have failed to listen?

Why this absence of emphasis on listening? There are several factors that have produced this situation. Listening—its behaviors, skills, and consequences—have been traditionally defined as belonging only to particular areas of faith and ministry, such as the contemplative tradition and pastoral counseling. A seminarian's introduction to listening skills, if any, usually comes with a summer or semester spent off campus in a clinical pastoral setting. While this setting certainly provides effective training, usually for listening to those *in extremis,* it is only a partial, therapeutic view of listening in the overall context of the multiple forms of listening expected vocationally from the minister.

In addition, the logocentric nature of the Christian tradition itself—its biblical, theological, and historical directions—have often eclipsed the role of listening in the activities of Christian ministry. When combined with the cultural assumptions undergirding a "can do" attitude, there is little time left for what many regard as the passive, even non-interactive, status of the listener.

Furthermore, the activity of silence as part of the listening process leaves many uncomfortable in a culture habituated to and over-whelmed with too many words.[3] One need only be present at worship in a congregation untrained and unaccustomed to silence to see the physical, nonverbal resistance to what they are hearing/listening to in worship during those moments that should be quiet ones.

There is also a gendered history related to listening that tends to relegate listening to some spheres and dismiss it from others. As cultural changes continue to occur, including the increasing numbers of women in theological education and ministry, the perceptions of the listener are changing. Studies show that listening is definitely gendered, leading to stereotypes about who listens best and how.[4]

What is at stake in cultivating listening skills for pastoral leaders today? The answer is, everything! As the Christian faith engages the new millennium, other pressures are bearing on pastoral leadership. Is it possible that our diversity, numbers, and pluralism are Spirit-inspired demands to address the other side of the communications coin before we speak anew? Many competing voices have entered the cultural faith fair, making it all the more urgent for pastoral leadership to hear those who struggle with multicultural perspectives, gender and sexuality issues, consumerism without guilt, and a search for meaning. A number of theologians are attempting to seize our attention in this regard, claiming that we are all called to a "keener recognition of the diversity, complexity, and ambiguity that have become the warp and woof of the common life we all share."[5] Such theologians have traced the desire for new perspectives, in part, to habits of listening formed in early childhood. Through a series of interviews, they traced the desire for new perspectives, in part, to habits of listening formed in early childhood:

> We were both amused and charmed to find an interesting pattern that we described as "listening from the stairway" in which children sitting at the top of stairways overheard adult conversations about community affairs that nourished their sense of connection to a larger world.[6]

Childhood listening is a keenly formative element in adult listening patterns that contribute to the current reconfiguring of global faith perspectives. Revisiting the memories of what was/is deemed important by the pastoral listener is essential stocktaking, part of the theological tradition of listening.

Across the entire spectrum of human life and faith, it is indeed time to revisit how listening informs ministry and to give serious thought to the seven-times repeated phrase, "Let anyone who has an ear listen to what the Spirit is saying to the churches" (Rev 2:7, 11, 17, 29—3:6, 13, 22).

## The Framework of Pastoral Listening

The remainder of the chapter will introduce the basic components of listening theory that form the argument of this book. First, I will present a definition of listening and a listening taxonomy developed by Wolvin and Coakley and based on speech communication research. Second, I will introduce a working definition of pastoral listening. Finally, I hope the reader will understand the rationale for listening well in pastoral ministry.

### Listening: What Is It?

Sadly, good listening skills are taken for granted by most pastoral leaders and yearned for by their people. Far from being "natural," gaining good listening skills takes an investment of time and education. Listening is so complex that the various branches of research in the field have not arrived at a shared, basic definition. In the midst of this confusion, it is easy to entertain mistaken notions of what it means to listen. Note the following common assumptions about this primary element of communication.

1. Listening and hearing are synonymous.
2. Listening competency develops naturally through daily practice.
3. Listening ability is largely dependent upon intelligence.
4. Listening and reading are the same process.
5. Listening is primarily a passive act.
6. Effective communication is the responsibility of the speaker.
7. Listening means agreement or obedience.
8. Actual listening is equated with perceived listening.[7]

All of these assumptions are incorrect. Agreeing with any of them has potential negative implications for pastoral leadership. For example, a church council gives careful and silent attention to a minister's major proposal for a new parish program. Believing that the council agrees with the plan, the minister then makes substantial commitments to a number of parties who need the program, only to find later that the council was still at the deliberative stage rather than at the point of approval. The council's ability to listen, while certainly laudatory, did not match the minister's, who assumed that silence indicated agreement with his proposal.

What happened during this listening event? First, the status of the spoken word, particularly on the part of the pastoral leader, tends to be weighted with high significance in ecclesial settings. It is a status that few lay people are willing to confront openly and without some major reservations. Buttressing this is an extensive historical and biblical emphasis on the sacredness of the word in both Hebrew scriptures and the New Testament. The Hebraic meanings of the verb "to listen" actually connote obedience to the listener at some levels (see chapter 2). Thus a number of elements—traditional, biblical, moral, and those pertaining to the use of pastoral authority—all contributed to the different hearings between minister and parishioners.

Another example will show that even adequate knowledge of listening dynamics does not necessarily clarify the complexities of the listening event, although it should deepen pastoral appreciation of it. A parish pastor requires confirmation students to take sermon notes. The intricacies of listening become obvious to the pastor after reading the students' notes. Some indicate they were listening to what the pastor believed she was saying; others wrote detailed notes that differed radically from what the pastor thought she preached; some students turned in notes that indicated little attention or confusion about what was proclaimed. Where does the "truth" of the listening event occur in such a context? (See chapter 6 on preaching and worship.)

Perhaps one of the most poignant occasions I experienced in pastoral ministry had to do with the third assumption—that listening ability is dependent on intelligence. One Sunday I preached at a service for a local California congregation. After I had handed the bread and wine to a member of the congregation who was mentally challenged, he smacked his lips, gave me a big smile, and said in a thrilled voice, "Thank you. Jesus serves the best meals of all!" He listened. He "got it," leaving me to wonder how much the rest of us had truly listened to the import of the communion liturgy.

## By Way of Introduction: Some Definitions

What, then, is listening? We may know its manifestations through what does or does not happen in our experience, but how does the field of communications regard listening? The following definitions may help forge working definitions of pastoral leadership listening.

In the early part of the twentieth century, one study defined listening as "the ability to understand spoken language."[8] A mid-century study defined listening as "the process of hearing, identifying, understanding, and interpreting spoken language."[9] Another researcher noted that it is "recognizing, and interpreting spoken symbols."[10] The International Listening Association (ILA), the primary research group in this field, periodically attempts to define listening. The definitions are always provisional, changing as new insights are added from researchers' work and experience. The ILA's current definition of listening (1996) reads: "the process of receiving, constructing meaning from, and responding to spoken and/or nonverbal messages."[11]

The pioneering work of Wolvin and Coakley provides a definition that seems the most comprehensive to date and provides the reference point for further discussion in this volume. Listening is "the process of receiving, attending to, and assigning meaning to aural and visual stimuli."[12] The definition includes the component of vision.

These sample definitions demonstrate that listening is a rich and complicated area of human response. One definition that is missing is "Christian listening." There is no such thing in one sense since listening is a commonly shared, creaturely activity and a learned, skills-based response. However, faith communities and their leaders can engage in listening with a clear understanding of what is at stake theologically as they develop listening skills. Daunting as that might be, the call to effective pastoral leadership nevertheless involves coming to terms with how one's ministry style meshes with the proposed definitions.

## A Methodology: The Wolvin-Coakley Listening Taxonomy

How does a basic definition of listening help our encounters with the types of listening that we experience in pastoral ministry? The answer is that the listening carried out in pastoral ministry occurs within the general framework of the various types of listening that everyone does in daily life. Listening is context dependent, but it may also be assigned a typology that demonstrates how listening in any context operates at several levels, either separately or in concert, enabling the listener to interpret what is being heard more effectively.

A helpful way to approach types of pastoral listening is through the lens of the Wolvin-Coakley typology of listening. Their typology will be used throughout the book to clarify pastoral listening habits and skills within the general forms of listening we all do, regardless of vocation. Because of the extensive research done by the authors in the field of listening, the use of their typology is just a sample of the in-depth resources they have assembled. Additionally, the forms of pastoral listening developed in this book will be defined both in agreement with and in contrast to these general listening modes.

Note that while the five types of listening build on one another, they can also occur simultaneously in different combinations. Each type makes specific physical, emotional, and intellectual demands of the listener. Investing in the wrong listening modality in a listening situation can create problems raging from the tragic to the comical. Wolvin and Coakley have identified these five types:

1. **Discriminative.** This is defined as "listening to distinguish auditory/and or visual stimuli" (56). This is listening at its most basic levels and involves the tasks of sorting out such things as sounds and noises. It includes paraverbal sounds like the volume, pitch, inflection, and pace of the speaker's voice. This kind of listening involves attention, concentration, and sensory acuity.

2. **Comprehensive.** Defined as "listening to understand the message." Three of the most important elements in this type of listening are memory, concentration, and vocabulary use (20). This type of listening demands attention, concentration, and understanding.

3. **Therapeutic.** This type of listening is the one most typically suggested to the speaker and listener when considering pastoral listening. It

is defined as "listening to provide a troubled sender with the opportunity to talk through a problem" (262). Listening of this sort demands attention, concentration, understanding, and empathy.

4. Critical. This type of listening is "listening to comprehend and then evaluate the message." Listening of this sort involves issues of truth, validity, and judgments about the ethos and credibility of both listener and speaker (308). The listener must bring to this form of listening attention, concentration, understanding, and evaluation.

5. Appreciative. This occurs when "listening [is] to obtain sensory stimulation or enjoyment through the works and experiences of others" (362). Here the listener must bring attention, concentration, and sensitivity.

With this taxonomy as a tool, we now turn to a working definition of what pastoral listening is about and, by implication, what it is not.

## Pastoral Leadership Listening: A Core Definition

If a case can be made for pastoral leadership listening as a special type of listening, what rules and faith perspectives govern it? Pastoral leadership listening is not exempt from the use of basic listening frameworks such as those proposed by the Wolvin-Coakley taxonomy. While these describe the various typical "how we might listen" approaches, pastoral listening takes these and other listening techniques into account from a particular perspective.

> *Good pastoral listening is governed by a basic knowledge and command of listening skills and structures. It is a theological activity, emerging from vocational and faith identity, present in all forms of ministry, and subject to pertinent societal and ecclesiastical boundaries. It can occur at sensory and nonsensory levels and is both individual and corporate in nature.*

This definition unfolds through various ministerial settings in the following pages. The reader may consider it as the interpretive prism through which different types of pastoral listening will be discussed. This definition is forged from the work of traditional and contemporary sources. Like definitions from the ILA and other listening research, it is a work-in-process.

## Why Bother?
## The Benefits of Good Pastoral Listening

What are the benefits and resources of an effective, skills-based foundation for pastoral ministry? One class member from the seminary listening course was only partially joking when he noted that whatever the benefits were professionally, his spouse was deeply appreciative of his increased ability to listen in and to their relationship!

The benefits of good pastoral listening involve the creative shaping of faith communities by establishing and maintaining healthy interpersonal, social, cultural, and ecclesial boundaries. Seriousness about this activity is important, for it is a direct theological witness to a crucial theological reality; that is, effective listening reflects the very nature of our personal and corporate relationships with a listening God.

Good pastoral listening is, among other things, also the act of Christian witness and defense for and against logomachies, those linguistic power structures of language that may either enhance and bless or betray and misinform members of the faith. Pastoral listening thereby deepens community ties and increases the flow of information, challenging and changing power imbalance. There is indeed a bravery and a responsibility about good pastoral listening. In a recasting of the Star Trek phrase, "It is committed to listening where no others are able or willing to listen!" Good listening intercommunally is significantly creative, even having teaching functions, and can extend from the community of faith through family, parish work, vocation, and corporate worship.

Truthful listening as a pastoral leader is costly. We might hear what we hoped we would not or could not. It may create relationships whose complexities daunt us. Good listening may take us to places with God and humanity that leave us with an entirely new set of questions and concerns. It is possible that good listening will open for each of us a window on our own lives that yields light and challenges the darkness—a sometimes exhausting dialogue. At its best, good listening will allow us to hear the passion, love, and complexity of ourselves and the world around us.

## Summary

Listening to others within the course of carrying out one's pastoral office is primarily an act of faith: a commitment to self, to God, and to others. This is the direction of good ministry; however, good listening is a learned behavior. Achieving better listening skills is a matter of education and practice. Unfortunately, traditional theological training has afforded the student almost no opportunities to learn to listen well.

Although there is no such thing as "Christian listening," effective pastoral leadership listening is subject to the same dynamics as general listening, but the process is nuanced in several unique ways through faith perspectives. The characteristics of good pastoral listening are forged by a combination of historical, biblical, and sociological facts, as well as human expectations. Good pastoral listening can only be termed that if it is thoroughly theological in orientation and meaning.

At the present time, no one has attempted to work out a theology that includes the act of listening in a key way. So the pastoral leader's listening efforts are still in search of a unified field of thought on this matter, although already existing forms of pastoral listening in specialized areas are characterized in a number of ways. Chapter 9 will draw together some of the beginning components of such a theology.

## For Discussion

1. Develop your own definition of listening. Is it consistent with what you emphasize in your pastoral leadership style (for example, characteristics of openness, willingness to dialogue, etc.)?

2. What training have you received in listening skills? How?

3. Who is the person who has listened best to you? The one who has been the worst at it? What has this meant for your life and ministry?

4. According to the Wolvin-Coakley taxonomy, are there any types of listening on which you concentrate the most? The least? Any that you have difficulty with or consciously shy away from?

5. Are the types of listening on which you focus, according to the taxonomy, commensurate with your ministry setting?

6. What does it mean for you to listen as a Christian?

7. In which ministry settings do you find it easiest to listen? The most difficult? Are there any listening situations that have "backfired" on you and, if so, why?

8. What personal factors block effective listening for you? Which ones enhance it?

9. List those elements that you would choose to add to the definition of pastoral listening and to the list of expectations related to pastoral listeners.

*Two*

# Listening and Hearing: The Scriptural Tradition

"Then from the cloud came a voice that said, 'This is my Son, my Chosen; listen to him!'"
—LUKE 9:35

The Gospel of Luke contains an ironic, amusing incident that follows the resurrection. The two disciples on the road to Emmaus unknowingly confront the risen Christ and ask: "Are you the only stranger in Jerusalem who does not know the things that have taken place there in these days?" (24:18). Luke's further description of the encounter inverts expectations of who listens and what they hear. The reader wants to cheer the disciples' naïve efforts to listen to the one who has heard it all! The incident stands directly within the biblical tradition of emphasizing the importance of listening.

The role of listening in the Christian theological tradition emerges from its primary expressions in both the Hebrew scripture and the New Testament. Neither presents anything resembling either a typology of listening or a developed theory of listening. Instead, they depict listening chiefly in terms of two opposing views that set listening and non-listening against one another. To listen well and truthfully is life, but refusing to listen is death. Life in all its fullness resides in the human capacity to willingly listen to God, while the refusal to listen denotes sin and finitude.

Over the following centuries, a handful of theologians occasionally referred to the dimensions of listening, but without much sense of its many contours and implications for ministry as a whole and often without direct reference to its roots in biblical theology. As a means of developing a contemporary theological rationale for pastoral listening leadership, this chapter will define the Hebrew and Greek words related to listening/hearing and offer examples of the Bible's contrasting views of listening and non-listening. This overview will highlight those aspects of the tradition useful in defining the listening work of present-day pastoral leaders.

## Scriptures and Listening

An examination of the communication emphases of the Christian tradition reveals the perennial tensions between word and image, between privileging hearing/listening over sight or the reverse. Christianity is a religion of revelation based on auditory presentations, communication forms, and evidence. It is also a religion based on image and on the incarnational representation of God in Jesus Christ. In one way, the focus of both hearing and seeing are unified in the person of Jesus Christ, and different traditions reflect an emphasis usually toward one or the other of these perspectives. One example would be the difference between a Protestant listening to a sermon and an Orthodox Christian's worship focused through an icon.

Biblical speech forms and emphases on receptivity toward the spoken word predominate in many traditions. They reveal God through prophecy, preaching, teaching, and various types of narrative speech. They are salvific forms of information about God and human community that emphasize God's activities. These forms are meant to be repeated and proclaimed. Certainly, in Christian evangelism and missionary work over the centuries, the proclamation of God's word has been central to the activities of the faithful. Most importantly, the narrative speech forms have been labeled as constitutive of true faith and therefore of life itself: "And how are they to hear without someone to proclaim him? . . . So faith comes from what is heard, and what is heard comes through the word of Christ" (Rom 10:14, 17).

The Christian faith in all its denominational aspects is in extensive possession of several well-developed "theologies of the Word,"[1] with their roots in biblical expressions of speech. The manner, modes, and rationale for listening, however, have received much less attention, despite their presence in Scripture.

Earlier, we emphasized the distinction Wolvin and Coakley make between hearing and listening. The two are not the same. The first connotes a mere apprehending of sound, while the latter makes sense of it according to certain emotional and intellectual responses; this book will maintain the distinction. The reader is cautioned, however, that scriptural texts often use the two words interchangeably as part of the complexities of original scriptural languages, translations, and cultural issues. For example, it would be difficult to imagine that the injunction to "Hear, O Israel . . ." (Deut 6:4, Mark 12:29) is meant only in the Wolvin-Coakley sense of registering sound without necessarily including making any sense of it! Based on context, the reader must decide on the intended meaning.

Hearing and listening are found in a variety of forms throughout both testaments. While theology has placed heavy emphasis on the word and its manifestations, it has done little to demonstrate how humanity might enact that word through listening (rather than through more words). The reason for that may be as simple as the central reality that sinful human beings have little interest in listening to God or to one another. On the other hand, reasons could be as complex as the interaction of the philosophical and religious traditions of Judaism, Hellenism, and Christianity, and the focus on language and the Word. Additionally, the shift away from a purely patriarchal perspective in many faith communities today has also redefined notions of power, speech, silence, and listening.[2]

## Listening in the Hebrew Scriptures

As mentioned earlier, listening or failing to listen is a matter of life or death in the Old Testament. The act of listening described in the Hebrew scriptures is both a physical event and a spiritual one. It is constitutive of the God-human relationship and is described in both positive and negative ways. The verbs for "listening" and "hearing" in Hebrew are *shāmaᶜ lᵉqôl* ("listen to the voice of") and *shāmaᶜ* ("hear"). In reading the word *listening,* it is important to remember that this verb "depends to a great degree on the context."[3] In other words, what is heard depends on who is saying it, to whom, and with what intention. From a divine perspective, God as listener "is concerned predominantly with calls, cries, laments, crying, asking, and wishing" on the part of human beings.[4]

The act of "listening," or "paying attention," connotes a cluster of meanings having to do with a whole range of responses connected with receptivity, understanding, and obedience. This latter response is particularly crucial and prevalent in the texts. Evidence of this Eastern Semitic interpretation of listening is found extrabiblically as well in the *Tales of the Arabian Nights*. When a person in authority gives a command, the subordinate's response is: "Hearing and obeying!"[5] So, conversely, the act of refusing to listen also connotes associations with spiritual deafness, hubris, and a broken relationship with God. The word "ear" is a metaphor for the whole person; it signifies instrumentality in either yielding to or refusing to hear God or humanity. Failure to hear results in separation from God and humanity; ultimately, it means that the non-listener dies.

How do the Hebrew scriptures talk about listening? Listening can be divided into several categories, including: (1) natural sounds, (2) listening as a human response to God's acts, (3) God's hearing of the people in its various forms, and (4) actions demonstrating the importance of listening. Since listening is a profoundly reciprocal activity, speaking or some form of action can preface or follow the act of listening.[6]

Undoubtedly, the most notable divine injunction to listen is the "Shema." This verse is found in Deuteronomy 6:4: "Hear, O Israel: The Lord is our God, the Lord alone." (Note the variants in different translations indicating the direction or content of what it is Israel is to hear.) This is a core command, and "[a]s the classical statement of monotheism and the highest confession of Judaism; it has become a martyr's cry and an identifying mark of Jews through the centuries."[7]

The understanding of the power of God's speech in the Hebrew scriptures, the necessity of listening and receiving in order to live, is carried into the writings of the New Testament—but with some additional nuances.

## Hearing and Listening in the New Testament

A large range of meanings and implications are tied to the New Testament's accounts of listening and must be considered within the word cluster: hearing, listening, ears, deaf(ness), voice, and obedience. The main verb for hearing/listening in the Greek is *akouō*.[8] The Greek also bears the same connotations of "proper-listening-as-obedience" as do its Semitic counterparts. (The same holds true for the connections between the Latin *obedires* [to obey] and *audire* [to hear/to listen]—important for a reading of Jerome's version of the biblical text.) An associated translation note for the history of English versions of the Bible is the use of the archaic word "harken" or "hearken." It is a hunting term referring to tracking animals that have lost but recovered the scent of their quarry.

The New Testament emphasis on hearing/listening is an attempt to encourage the listener to hear the good news, to listen to preaching and instruction for understanding and for life. It expands the Hebrew meaning of hearing/listening to indicate commitment to the one being listened to. In other words, true human listening is true salvation in Jesus Christ. Listening is more than obedient cognition: it is obedience to a relationship and to a person.

The role of listening in the New Testament shows itself in the theological areas of salvation, ecclesiology, and eschatology.

**Salvation.** As with Old Testament materials, right listening/hearing in the New Testament results in life not death. Perhaps the major narrative describing the links among Jesus, listening, and salvation is found in the descriptions of the transfiguration that conclude not with "See!" but with "This is my Son, my Chosen; listen to him!" (Luke 9:35).[9] In particular, the fourteenth chapter of John's Gospel depicts Jesus repeatedly ascribing what the disciples hear, not to him but to his Father.

Undoubtedly one of the key passages for identifying the instrumentality of salvation—the ear, the capacity to hear—is Romans 10:17: "So faith comes from what is heard, and what is heard comes through the word of Christ." Hearing is the means of obtaining salvation. John's Gospel speaks intimately of that in a pastoral metaphor: "My sheep hear my voice. I know them, and they follow me" (John 10:27).

As do the Hebrew scriptures, Jesus continually urges the people to listen and points out the spiritual peril of those who do not. Periodically he even expresses his frustration with the disciples' inability to hear/listen. The failure to listen is equated with the refusal to understand and, by extension, the loss of one's salvation.[10] One of the most extended passages related to this is found in the thirteenth chapter of Matthew.

The passage is double-edged. First, it uses the parable of the sower to distinguish those who listen and are saved from the types of hearers who do not listen and are not saved. By using the parable form, Jesus' explanation instructs the disciples in the complexities of listening. What is often vital is not necessarily immediately apparent. In fact, listening to God involves searching for God within the veil of language. The very use of the parable form itself in relaying this information comes as a speech form that both hides and reveals God. Listening to the parable actually invites the listener to enter even more deeply into what it means to listen and live. It is a speech form that invites dialogue, engagement, questioning, and enlightenment. As Matthew recounts it, Jesus prefaces the parable with Isaiah's prophetic words regarding God's power to deafen the people's ability to listen. Jesus places his listeners in a more fortunate light: "But blessed are . . . your ears, for they hear" (Matt 13:16).

**Ecclesiology.** Listening is connected with the development of discipleship in the early church in several ways. The birth of the church begins with the Pentecost experience of a "designer God," namely, the people hear God in their own language (Acts 2:6). The source of true knowledge and faith is born out of hearing and recognizing God's voice through a variety of inspired human speech forms.

The growth of the church and fellowship depends on listening to the witness of other faith communities. Paul reassures the Ephesians that he will remember them because "I have heard of your faith in the Lord Jesus and your love toward all the saints" (Eph 1:15). One of the specific measurements of the growing church's well-being was emphasized through Paul's interesting metaphor of the body of Christ in 1 Corinthians 12. This organic, lively metaphor is prefaced with his observation that his listeners had been previously "led astray to idols that could not speak" (v. 2). That is, they worshiped that which could not listen or hear them and thus could not respond. The metaphor of the body of Christ gives a very different picture of and to the worshiper: it is one of life and reciprocal listening.

Paul warns, however, of inequities and imbalance. The grotesque results of a misshapen or misused body include the implications of this comment: "And if the ear would say, 'Because I am not an eye, I do not belong to the body,' that would not make it any less a part of the body. . . . If the whole body were hearing, where would the sense of smell be?" (vv. 16-17). In this example the implication is strong that listening unaccompanied by faithful interaction renders the body of Christ useless.

**Eschatology.** Despite vivid imagery of the end times used in different places throughout the New Testament, an examination of the visual elements shows that the emphasis also includes the auditory at pivotal points. The preaching of God's good news is the prelude to the end: "And this good news of the kingdom will be proclaimed throughout the world, as a testimony to all the nations; and then the end will come" (Matt 24:14). "Heaven and earth will pass away, but my words will not pass away" (Matt 24:35).

The Book of Revelation signifies for many a collection of violent, unusual images, yet it too is characterized by repeated demands to attend to the voice of prophecy and testimony. The following phrases typify the book's contents: "Let anyone who has an ear listen to what the Spirit is saying to the churches" (Rev 2:7). Perhaps one of the most stunning verses appears at the beginning of the eighth chapter as the witness hears the following: "When the Lamb opened the seventh seal, there was silence in heaven for about half an hour" (Rev 8:1). It is reasonable to ask what was being listened to during that time.

The issue of meaningful sounds in Revelation prompts the reader to think about what the sounds signify. Throughout the book, the sound of the seven angels with the seven trumpets signifies the beginning of the end. The eighteenth chapter contains a peculiar litany of the sounds that humanity will no longer hear after the final day: the sounds of music, of daily work (the millstone), and of human relationships as symbolized by the voices of the bride and bridegroom. The book's final verses conclude with multiple invitations, including this one: "And let everyone who hears say, 'Come'" (Rev 22:17).

## Summary

A continuity of theological direction and concern about listening is expressed in both testaments. Listening or failing to listen to God means the difference between salvation, life, and spiritual and physical death. The listening, however, is not unidirectional. God, as one who speaks and one who remains silent, always confronts the human as potential listener.

The Hebrew scriptures describe the divine-human relationship in anthropomorphic terms: like human beings, God is capable of choosing to listen or not to listen. Human faith and well-being must be constructed on this reciprocal speaking/listening relationship with God. The relationship can be either positive or negative in nature; it is both practical and formal (for example, liturgical) in nature. The Hebrew scriptures also describe the divine-human relationship in terms of listening or deafness in a way that is highly symbolic of the fluctuations of humanity's relationship with God. God chooses to shut God's ears occasionally! Likewise, the manner in which human beings listen to one other and to their physical world also describes literally and metaphorically the extent to which they will either thrive or die.

The descriptions of listening in the New Testament continue this tradition of the divine-human listening/speaking relationship and add other dimensions. However, hearing God's word according to New Testament sources occurs "in a very different sense from that of Judaism with its exclusive emphasis on teaching."[11] Listening in the New Testament is a *mediated* relationship. Jesus, Son of God, continues the listening relationship of humanity with God modeled in the Hebrew scriptures. There is, however, a more intense scrutiny of the various roles of listening: it is the medium of salvation; it is the catalyst in constructing the church and its relationships; and, despite the primacy of eschatological imagery and vision, it remains the believer's means of responding in faith to God and of remaining faithful to the end.

Scripture presents listening, like salvation, as both simple and complex. Hearing God's word may involve approaching language differently, that is, with an openness to attending to sacred speech in numerous ways through the infinite play of language. Jesus himself warned the disciples in his preface to the parable of the sower that there is hearing and then there is listening. An example of this is the attention the believer may direct to the parables as a form of an invitation to salvation. Accepting the multilayered nature and mystery of this parabolic God language means that the act of human listening should never be regarded complacently—because, in human terms, it is never fully completed. Most importantly, listening in the New Testament always points to listening to God's word in the person of Jesus Christ. In him, hearing, listening, silence, and speech all converge for the benefit of the listener's salvation.

What, then, are the implications of this biblical material for the development of strong listening practices in ministry? Scripture witnesses to several things that include listening as a characteristic of the divine-human relationship: true listening as salvific, listening appropriately as the means to deepening and expanding Christian community, and the expression of the Gospel in multiple contexts. Jesus' teachings in particular point out how arduous the listening task can be. Merely hearing something is insufficient, but listening well is life itself.

## For Discussion

1. What elements in today's global setting necessitate listening in different ways? Do you have any examples from your own community?

2. What characteristics would describe the believer-listener? What actions?

3. Are there any differences in emphasis related to listening between Hebrew scripture and the New Testament?

4. What are the various consequences of understanding listening in the biblical sense of "listening as obeying"?

5. What liturgical sounds prompt listening to God and to the faith community?

6. Which faith traditions have emphasized the visual, and how do they differ in emphases compared to those that emphasize the aural?

7. How would you describe good pastoral listening in relationship to the issues about listening in the biblical record?

8. What cultural and personal ongoing distractions today prevent effective pastoral listening as defined in the Bible?

*Three*

# Pastoral Listening:
# The Theological Heritage

The confessor should always be ready and willing to hear the confessions of the faithful when they make a reasonable request.
— *The Rites of the Catholic Church*

If one asks whether such a "theology of communicating" exists neatly organized, clearly stated, and bound in leather, the answer is No.
— Seward Hiltner, *Preface to Pastoral Theology*

The tradition of the pastoral listener ranges from Jesus asking, "What is it you want me to do for you?" (Mark 10:36) to the one listening to the penitent in the confessional or pastor's study. This chapter will explore three perspectives on the pastoral listener: first, some of the major, general expectations people have of the pastoral listener; second, the history of pastoral listening practices, particularly as evidenced in the Sacrament of Reconciliation; and finally, the contemporary evolution of pastoral listening as viewed through the Wolvin-Coakley category of "therapeutic listening."

## Expectations of Pastoral Listeners

Participants in the seminary listening course created a list of what they had experienced in terms of people's expectations of their pastoral listening stance. They noted a variety of interrelated issues including the ethos of the pastoral listener and the potential range of audiences and topics involved in such listening:

- Ministers are known, or wish to be known, as model listeners. They are "typed" as available listeners for their constituencies and for the general public. They listen interrelatedly in a network of relationships and community responsibilities. Sometimes this pastoral listening is expected to be "on behalf of" those groups or persons with little or no voice. In other words, ministers are expected to listen watchfully, as advocates who are alert to change in the private and public sectors.

- What ministers listen to include key hot topics, whether these are private or communal. They listen to these as people who are informed listeners, operating under the rubric of confidentiality, and listen disinterestedly and ethically. Confessional speaking is regarded by those confessing to be confidential hearing; trust forms the environment for true hearing. This means ministers are expected to listen with no desire to inflict pain, prior judgments, or for personal gain.

- Ministers are also expected to listen in order to discern and bring clarity to often-chaotic human situations which [that] require a sense of timing (including the use of silence). They also demonstrate that their listening has goals outside themselves; in other words, ministers are expected to do intermediary, vicarious listening—on behalf of God, for God's sake, incarnationally.

- Ministers are also perceived by the speakers as individuals shaped by various faith structures; that is, they will listen from particular doctrinal and ecclesial perspectives and not others. This includes the growing awareness that pastoral listening is gendered. How, what, why, and to whom they listen is focused and shaped by the gender relationships brought to the listening event. Above all else, ministers are expected to listen for and to God in their own lives as a preliminary form of listening to all others forms of listening.

## Confessional Listening

One of the types of listening that the minister engages in, according to the "therapeutic" mode of Wolvin-Coakley, can be termed "confessional listening"—pastoral listening that occurs either in corporate or individual settings. Some judicatories have even established crisis listening teams, sending them to listen to severely conflicted congregations. Scriptural, doctrinal, and professional guidelines support this form of listening.

Scriptural references to confession of sin between individuals have communal implications as well as personal meanings. "So when you are offering your gift at the altar, if you remember that your brother or sister has something against you, leave your gift there before the altar and go; first be reconciled to your brother or sister, and then come quickly and offer your gift (Matt 5:23-24).[1] The writer of James specifies different prayers, one of which is: "Therefore confess your sins to one another, and pray for one another, so that you may be healed" (James 5:16).

Images of a priest listening to confession are public, widespread, and part of the secular fascination with religious practices. Confessional hearing is often a quasi-religious experience, too; for the general public it is sometimes voyeuristic in nature, as exhibited in magazines like *True Confessions* or in a televised presidential admission of wrongdoing.[2]

Sacramental acts of listening have been portrayed in films many times over the years, defining the ministerial role for the secular audience. Hearing confessions is depicted in movies such as *I Confess,* the extended confessional sequence in *House of the Spirits,* and *The Priest.*[3] All of these present the priest as listener. The listening event of the confessional is the symbolic and dramatic center of each of the movies. Here listening and speaking appear significantly at the intersection of good and evil, sin and human struggle, and the revelation of changing truths. The ecclesiastical context signifies mystery, choice, divine "overhearing," and the drama of high-stakes listening. The listening is also framed by nonverbal commentary, including who is listening and how the information is received.

Confessing to a pastoral listener has occasioned humor, terror, legal consequences, and new freedom for the penitent. It has a long history in the church and has been formed by numerous canon laws, experience, and liturgical directives in both Roman Catholic and Protestant circles. A reading of this complex history must take into consideration topics such as absolution, contrition, penance, the confessor, the power of the keys, secrecy, and corporate and private confession. Since Vatican II, the Sacrament of Reconciliation has undergone a number of significant changes for speaker and listener.[4] It is also finding renewed attention in Protestant circles. One offshoot of this has emerged through services of the Word for healing.[5]

The early church met the biblical mandates to confess in a formal way by establishing the sacrament of penance.[6] Instructional manuals for confessors were published over the centuries, instructing the priest listener on listening and speaking skills for eliciting confessions. At the time of the Reformation, debates intensified around the role and liturgical significance of this activity of confession and absolution.[7]

Protestant engagement with this activity continued with the writings of Luther, Melanchthon, and Calvin. Luther maintained that penance was a sacrament, although he eventually anchored it in a return to baptism, thus drawing ambiguous lines regarding his sacramental theology.[8] Melanchthon also held that penance was a sacrament.[9] However, Calvin denied that it was.[10] The Protestant reformers described confession, forgiveness, and absolution as a means of grace and emphasized tradition through the biblical notion of the "power of the keys." Luther's "Small Catechism" contains a form for private confession.[11] Except for special occasions, often during the seasons of Lent or Advent or by request, individual confession does not play a major role in Protestant church life today; usually confession exists primarily in its corporate forms.

Max Thurian, a Reformed theologian, has written an excellent book on confession.[12] Protestants unfamiliar with the rich history and dynamics of this activity in the life of the church will find helpful historical and theological information therein along with a variety of confessional rites. As Thurian notes, Saint Augustine and Saint Leo were the first to demand the *sigillum confessionis* (the seal of the confession). Thurian speaks of how this seal affects the pastoral listener completely in both verbal and nonverbal ways.

> It is the duty of the confessor to keep with the utmost scrupulousness the promise which the Church requires of him at his consecration, to keep secret the confessions which may be made to him for the quieting of conscience. This is only a matter of refraining from repeating a private confession, which goes without saying. His whole attitude, his words and gestures, as well as any measures he may be called upon to take elsewhere with regard to a person who has made his confession to him, must be such that they will in no way betray the confession that has been made.[13]

This passage is interesting because nonverbal behaviors are not only remarked upon—they are understood as potential betrayers of confidences outside of the confessional, giving clues to the hearing/listening setting itself.

Confessors/pastoral listeners have changed in character and perspective with the move to the ordination of women in the twentieth century. As a result, some liturgical rites for confession have shifted in content and direction as well. One significant set of exchanges between confessor and penitent is a liturgical structure established for women who have been sexually abused.[14] Respondents to a confessor's questions have the option of two or more answers. Another rite for women encourages listening to and forgiving women's sins through nonverbal activities and silence.[15]

## Pastoral Listening: Textual Tributaries

Confession of sins is only one part of the pastoral listening tradition. Over the centuries, pastoral care and the types of listening attendant upon it have gone by several names: "the cure of souls," "pastoral theology," "pastoral counseling." Each of these terms means something somewhat different from the others. The first one continues to influence the Christian tradition today through a variety of classic manuals and pastoral letters by Augustine, John Cassian, Richard Baxter, Jeremy Taylor, and Martin Luther. The latter two terms represent developments in pastoral counseling, pastoral theology, and hybrids of the two. Because of the complexity of these fields, their developments, detractors, supporters, and trends, only the issue of the presence or absence of listening skills in well-known representative texts will be discussed in the following pages. (Refer to Appendix A to see how these and other texts talk about listening.)

Several core assumptions span all the texts regarding the role of listening in pastoral work. All the texts understand the pastor as counselor; maintain a basic theological perspective on speaking and hearing; have a particular understanding of some form of a "theology of the Word of God" and how that corresponds to human use of language in counseling; and value the knowledge of and importance of communication skills. Developments in the field of communications implicitly and explicitly govern each book's ideas about listening.

Dietrich Bonhoeffer's *Spiritual Care,* for example, is heavily dependent on the Reformation tradition: the Word of God, the Bible as presented in the public Sunday sermon, is the main delivery system for pastoral care. No definition of listening is offered: one is expected to listen in this way: "It must become clear that everything necessary for our help is to be found in the Word of God and that it is essential for us to listen to the Word."[16] The certainty and power of the Word allow no substantial development of the tasks of human listening. The pastor-as-listener is absent from Bonhoeffer's approach to pastoral care, except, of course, as a conduit of the Word. Some of the pastor/counselee dialogues simply return the counselee to the attention of his or her sinfulness—regardless of the pain expressed or the question asked. In other words, the pastor must listen only to the Word of God for the counselee. Bonhoeffer's judgments of counselees who are troubled, struggling, or unable to respond are harsh, since their attitudes, according to Bonhoeffer, emerge from their reluctance to appropriate God's Word.

One of the early pioneers in the field of pastoral theology, Seward Hiltner is the author of *Pastoral Counseling* and *Preface to Pastoral Theology*.[17] In the former, listening is presumed but neither defined nor discussed as a counseling skill. In the latter book, there is also no information about listening. However, Hiltner does have one section and one chapter entitled "Communicating." He notes that recent years have brought new communication studies: "Very little of this work has so far been assimilated, at least to the depth available, in Christian theories of communicating the gospel."[18] His understanding of communication focuses on the verbal responses the pastoral counselor makes in reference to the Word of God in its various manifestations.

Howard Clinebell's 1984 edition of *Basic Types of Pastoral Care and Counseling* discusses listening in three pages in the context of therapeutic listening ("healing").[19] Little is said about actual listening skills, although he does speak of both the outcome of good listening and the problems the counselor may have that could block it. Clinebell has two definitions for listening: "The art of *reflective empathic listening* is essential in all caring and counseling. The pastor attempts to listen to feelings (as well as words) including *feelings* that are between the lines, too painful to trust to words."[20] An enlargement of this definition reads, "Empathic listening is active listening demanding an emotional investment in the other and relative openness to one's own feelings."[21] His other definition reads: "As counselors listen *in depth* . . . This kind of listening is 'disciplined listening'—focused on what seems to have the most feeling, meaning, energy and pain."[22]

A pastoral care book by Paul W. Pruyser, *The Minister as Diagnostician: Personal Problems in Pastoral Perspective,* contains a rich cache of information on the historical paths that pastoral counseling has taken and the theological foundations of its future.[23] Despite a chapter entitled "Language in the Pastoral Relationship," the book is silent on the role of listening.

In *The Christian Pastor,* pastoral theologian Wayne Oates does not index "listening" or "hearing."[24] He mentions Douglas Steere's work, *On Listening to Another,* only in reference to pastoral vulnerability and not to listening.[25] In a section entitled "The Deeper Levels of Pastoral Care," he discusses "The Phase of Listening and Exploration."[26] After a three-page discussion of the three points, his definition of listening is summed up in this way: "These are the three significant meanings of the listening ministry—hearing what the person says, letting the person do the talking, and actively encouraging the person to talk."[27]

Thomas C. Oden's *Pastoral Theology: Essentials of Ministry* covers issues related to the pastoral office, the role of the clergy, pastoral counsel, and crisis situations.[28] References to listening as a component of these elements is almost completely lacking with the exception of one page devoted to "the listening ministry," and that is actually about establishing a trust relationship. No mention is made of the nature, necessity, or function of pastoral listening skills apart from strictly theological considerations.

Another major, recent writer in the field of pastoral theology is Charles V. Gerkin, author of *Prophetic Pastoral Practice: A Christian Vision of Life Together.*[29] Despite an excellent analysis of cultural readings, metaphor, and hermeneutics (à la Gadamer) on vocation, the author says nothing about the role listening plays in his presentation of story, culture, and faith. All the elements for several vital listening venues are established, but the why and how of listening to them is absent and creates a gap in the argument.

A recent book on pastoral ministry, *The Arts of Ministry: Feminist-Womanist Approaches,* is a collection of essays whose conclusion states:

> *The writers focus on listening deeply* to diverse voices of the people whose experience is at stake in these constructions of theories and practices of ministry, and helping people to find language for their experience that is meaningful and transforming. . . . Privileging the hearing of women's voices and experiences is common to all the chapters.[30]

While this statement is general, definitions, functions, and the skills of listening are strangely absent considering the cross-cultural nature of the essays. However, given the "coming to voice" of the groups represented, speaking rather than listening is perhaps the desired methodology. Paradoxically, the stated desire to "listen deeply" potentially conflicts with the allowance of new voices from unheard communities.

One of the best recent works on pastoral counseling, *The Skilled Helper: A Problem-Management Approach to Healing* by Gerard Egan, focuses more specifically on pastoral listening.[31] The second part of the book concentrates on communication skills. Here Egan distinguishes between the field of communications and theology. He defines listening as having four components: "Complete listening involves four things: first, observing and reading the client's nonverbal behavior—posture, facial expressions, movement, tone of voice, and the like. Second, listening to and understanding the client's verbal messages. Third, listening to the context; that is, to the whole person in the context of the social settings of his or her life. Fourth, listening to sour notes; that is, things the client says that may have to be challenged."[32] Egan's fifth chapter is entitled "Communication Skills I: Attending and Listening." The materials on listening are grounded in a knowledge of nonverbal behavior and of good communicative listening skills. Egan's discussion is interesting because he clearly separates listening skills from some of the older designations of listening-as-empathic-listening. He notes the confusion people have about "empathy as a way of being and empathy as a communication process or skill."[33] The chapter also contains subsections on what Egan calls "The Shadow Side of Listening to Clients" and "Listening to Oneself." Egan carries the issue of listening into client work and urges that the pastoral counselor encourage the client to "develop active listening skills."[34] This work is by far the most congruent with the Wolvin-Coakley framework concerning the definition, use, and acquisition of listening skills.[35]

# What the Written Tradition Reveals about Listening

The previous survey reveals an evolution of thinking regarding pastoral listening in twentieth-century materials. First, traditionally listening has focused on listening to the Word of God by both pastor and counselee. Earlier works concentrated on the sufficiency of "the Word," to the extent that it supplanted any need for attention to human communications perspectives. Bonhoeffer's approach is perhaps the most significant example of this and remains the major perspective of some faith communities.

A second stage of thinking about listening coincides with changes in the broad field of communications over the last thirty years. Pastoral theological works acknowledged the process of human listening, but always with theological intent and with little if any reference to the field of communications. Two phrases frequently used without explanation or definition were "empathic listening" (combining an attitude and a skill) and "the listening ministry" (combining a skill with a vocation). In some sense, this demonstrates a movement away from dominating "theologies of the Word" toward exploration of other avenues of communication, but no clear distinctions were made, nor were instructions given about developing listening skills.

Finally, a third stage seems to have emerged. Pastoral texts mention listening for a number of reasons: as a means to other ends (such as interview structuring), as part of attending behaviors, or as a communication tool and skill. To some extent the "skills language" has now replaced or runs parallel to listening as a form of affective response. Listening has assumed other definitions outside the skills area as well. Taken broadly, it can be a method of doing pastoral theology, for example, a type of meta-level listening to other areas of thought such as literary theory, hermeneutics, and theology (see Gerkin). There is a new awareness of community contexts not commonly attended to by the pastoral listener.

In summary, the literature in pastoral theology and counseling has tended until recently to concentrate more on speaking than on listening, whether it is speaking the Word of God, the speech of the counselee, or enumerating the proper and improper ways the counselor verbalizes responses. Overall, little if anything has been said about listening skills in most of the literature of the past fifty years. Discussion of listening skills as a central framework rather than as part of conversation or interview techniques is generally absent. Texts presume the reader knows all about listening—its meaning, functions, techniques, problems, and benefits. Engaging the one speaking (the client) in the process of also learning listening skills—or at least being aware of their exercise—is explicitly mentioned only in Egan and in a handful of other works. In effect, the survey demonstrates the need for more specific instruction in the skills and practice of listening.

## Summary

The theological tradition of listening reveals that those who speak confidentially with pastors do so within a general cultural set of expectations. Such expectations have been fostered by centuries of public experience with ministers whose work included an emphasis on listening framed within the liturgical tradition of the sacrament of penance. With the development of pastoral care approaches, a variety of terms have been applied over the centuries to the types of listening involved in the minister and speaker relationship. Each has overlapping, though different, histories, resources, and approaches. The assumption has been that pastors have good listening skills, despite the contrary evidence that such information is absent in pastoral literature.

In the twentieth century a shift has taken place, corresponding to developments in the field of communications; listening is understood to be an important skill with many facets. Skills language is now part of, or parallel to, the theological concerns that predominated in earlier pastoral care books

Clearly much work remains in giving listening the predominant place it deserves in theological practice. It is essential to reestablish the biblical perspectives on listening and to reassess how these should inform work on listening further in the pastoral theological tradition.

## For Discussion

1. What have been your own experiences with the set of pastoral listening expectations described at the beginning of this chapter?

2. What has been your formal theological education in engaging in the "cure of souls"? Is listening to confession a part of this activity, and what has been your experience with it?

3. How do you view the act of confession in your own pastoral practice? How do your own practices correspond with those of your denomination?

4. Have any particular pastoral theologians had a major influence on the way you listen in pastoral settings? Who are they and why have they been influential for you?

5. Have you ever read any of the major pastoral manuals related to the cure of souls from the pastoral literature of the past centuries? If so, which ones have you read? What did you learn from them?

*Four*

# Listening and the Law

We should keep our word, honor confidences, tell the truth. . . . And
we should also respect the mystery of things, the surprises. . . . What
love and justice require will not always be clear.
                                 —William W. Rankin, *Confidentiality and Clergy*

I f you were to construct a personal listening style survey, what would
be your answer to this question: What do I know about the legal
issues pertaining to my listening skills and settings?

In addition to the scriptural and pastoral traditions of listening, a rel-
atively new element has now entered the conversation about what listening means to pastoral leaders. That new element is the law. Whether
that means ecclesiastical codes, local, state, or federal laws, listening
venues are receiving new scrutiny by lawmakers. The formerly privileged confessional now has other ears in addition to pastoral ones.

## The Laws of Listening

Good basic listening skills, while unchanging to some extent, today
depend on their implementation in different ways due to the development of a new awareness legally, professionally, and personally in terms
of the pastoral-parishioner relationship. This new alertness to the
implications of listening is increasing as individuals and groups pon-
der the problems that work against good listening.

The reasons for inappropriate or inadequate listening skills are
numerous. The listener may be desensitized to the issue by choice or
by chance. Some of the issues raised may be outside the emotional,

experiential, or intellectual range of the listener—every listener is possessed of personal biases and blind spots. The usual factors that prompt a poor communication environment may also deter good listening, such as fatigue, inattention, boredom, or an inappropriately charged emotional atmosphere. These have all become significant factors in a particularly painful issue in many church judicatories, both Roman Catholic and Protestant, because historical vocational imperatives regarding the relational forms of ministry have been violated occasionally, resulting in damaging publicity and legal consequences.

What does it mean to listen in these potentially jeopardized circumstances? By "jeopardized circumstances" we refer not only to the potential for legal problems in counseling/listening settings for the pastoral listener, but also for those individuals who come for counseling who may be themselves in fragile circumstances. These circumstances may be ongoing or unexpected. The listening in such situations may be fraught with tension, confusion, and possibly even physical danger. The pastoral listener may be summoned unexpectedly to listen with little preparation for what she or he may encounter.

No human issue is exempt from pastoral listening. Besides the usual round of parish issues, others may demand more immediate attention: significant spiritual crises, suicide attempts/prevention, counseling those who are infected with sexually transmitted diseases, child abuse, domestic violence, and counseling those who are dealing with the realities of sexual orientation. (This latter reality has seen public transgressions of confidential listening that have been given a name, "outing.")

These types of therapeutic/counseling encounters also present legal issues that have not been present in former years or, if present, the accountability factors have not been as demanding. Today, however, those seeking help may claim that they have not been heard, thus causing damage and even death for themselves or others because of perceived inappropriate pastoral listening. Those who are second and third parties to the original speakers may also claim damages against faith communities and their leaders in this regard. If there are legal obligations and strictures from state or federal courts regarding any of these situations, the minister will need to decide how to signal a dual set of obligations to the speaker—wishing to hear pastorally but also needing to alert the speaker to the legal implications of what is being shared. The pastoral listener must decided both in an overall way and in specific situations whether or not confidentiality issues should be discussed beforehand or if the trust factor is dependable enough between listener and speaker to ensure confidentiality in an implicitly assumed manner. Counseling liability insurance is now available to congregations and has both negative aspects and positive benefits. While such insurance can offer protection to congregations when staff members violate parishioners; on the other hand, those with unscrupulous motives can also bring suit against such churches that they know hold such insurance policies.

Two major, interrelated, and seemingly contradictory realities relate to clergy listening and the law: (1) legally mandated disclosure of information that can be damaging to others if kept private, and (2) maintaining pastoral confidentiality. In the words of Ecclesiastes, the responses heard or discerned in counseling mean that the clergy listener must know the difference between a "time to keep silence and a time to speak" (3:7b). The minister, caught between speaking out or remaining silent, may face a catch-22 situation.

## Listening and Disclosure

An additional burden placed on today's listening clergy is the legal demand of disclosure of information if people's lives are endangered. This can involve domestic violence, child abuse, threats of violence against one or more people, and suicide threats.

The laws are complex regarding clergy disclosure. Clergy need to acquaint themselves with the laws of such disclosure in their own geographic area. As an example of the legal morass, in the author's state of Pennsylvania, the general law pertaining to revealing transgressions related to child abuse reads:

> Persons who, in the course of their employment, occupation or practice of their profession, come into contact with children shall report or cause a report to be made in accordance with the Section 23 Pa. C.S.A. #6311 (relating to reporting procedure) when they have reasonable cause to suspect on the basis of their medical, professional, or other training and experience, that a child coming before them in their professional or official capacity is an abused child.[1]

This is the general law. Note the following exception:

> Clergy do not have a legal duty to report child abuse if that infor-
> mation is obtained in a "privileged communication." [42 Pa.
> C.S.A. #5943 (1990)]

In 1995 this statute was amended:

> No clergyman . . . who while in the course of his duties has
> acquired information from any person secretly and in confidence
> shall be compelled, or allowed without consent of such person, to
> disclose that information in any legal proceeding, trial or investi-
> gation before any government unit.

The clergy listener, then, must decide to handle potentially danger-
ous situations for self, for congregation, and for those being counseled.
Prior to any problems, it would be wise for the clergy listener to meet
with the leadership of the parish and discuss overall understandings of
confidentiality, counseling approaches, and views on liability factors.

One source that can provide up-to-date information for ministers
on the law is the quarterly journal *Church Law and Tax Report*.[2] There
are also a growing number of books on the legal elements of pastoral
listening.[3] Interestingly, the legal arena does not provide the only legal
challenges to pastoral ministry standards regarding listening practices
and responses—insurance companies do so as well. Large payouts for
cases involving pastoral abuse of parishioners have prompted companies to make policy changes.

Because of these issues, it seems all the more appropriate that parish
leadership develop ways to educate themselves and their parishioners
in good listening skills. Whenever possible, these listening skills
should be defined for those in therapeutic settings with pastors as a
way to establish boundaries for all parties concerned.

## Listening and Confidentiality

One way of approaching listening and the law is by gaining a thorough
knowledge of the ecclesial standards established by most denominations that govern the hearing of clergy in counseling settings. Violation
of confidences by clergy listeners has caused repeated problems

throughout the church. These violations can range from subtle inferences concerning privileged information to outright public discussion of private information. The abuse of pastoral power and the pastoral office are at the heart of such unfair disclosures. This issue has been officially framed within larger views of clergy codes of conduct and standards of professional ethics.

The minister-listener in any structured ecclesial judicatory probably has some notion of the intersection of legal and church codes of behavior as they pertain to therapeutic listening. As an example of this, in the author's own Lutheran (Evangelical Lutheran Church in America [ELCA]) structures, ecclesial codes contain a three-tiered official documentation of listening and confidentiality injunctions and expectations.

First, there is the ordination service's charge to "care for God's people, bear their burdens and do not betray their confidence."[4]

The second injunction is found in "Vision and Expectations," a document that serves as a code of pastoral conduct.

> The church expects that its ordained ministers will honor and respect privileged communication, particularly within the context of individual confession and absolution, and will not disclose such communications except with the express permission of the person who has confided it or if the person is perceived to intend great harm to self or others.[5]

Third, in the ELCA's churchwide constitution, the same statement with some historical background is added:

> In keeping with the historic discipline and practice of the Lutheran church and to be true to a sacred trust inherent in the nature of the pastoral office, no ordained minister of this church shall divulge any confidential disclosure received in the course of the care of souls or otherwise in a professional capacity, nor testify concerning conduct observed by the ordained minister while working in a pastoral capacity, except with the express permission of the person who has given confidential information to the ordained minister or who was observed by the ordained minister, or if the person intends great harm to self or others.[6]

If no such guidelines exist for the pastoral listener in his or her ministry setting, then the next step is to learn what public, legal codes—if any—bear on such matters. This area of the law is complicated, changeable, and subject to wide interpretation. It touches on areas of confidentiality, divulgence of confidences, professional ethics, criminal intent or activity, and codes of conduct. Ministerial listeners should never attempt to "go it on their own" when significant questions arise. It is always wise to seek the advice of an attorney.

Perhaps one of the best sources for what binds the pastoral listener is *Confidentiality and Clergy: Churches, Ethics, and the Law* by William Rankin.[7] It contains an extended section on the history of confession and concludes with some needed but chilling advice on what steps to take should a minister become involved in litigation. Other texts on this subject are worth pursuing for those whose ministries are significantly tied to counseling and listening.

## Summary

Pastoral listening is receiving new attention from several sources that are legal, ecclesiastical, and social in nature. As a result, ministers should be acquainted with those laws that govern therapeutic listening, ecclesiastical and civil, in their venues. This also means that the minister will make choices to avoid listening settings that may jeopardize self or others.

Legal matters governing clergy listening fall into two areas: disclosure of information and confidentiality. "To tell or not to tell" is a dilemma faced often by ministers. In some cases the answer is an obvious yes, and in others an obvious no. The legal issues come to the fore in the ambiguous area between these.

The wisest step a minister and a faith community can take to ensure good listening and the avoidance of legal problems is to provide listening education for ministers and for those to whom they minister.

## For Discussion

1. How does your faith community regard the issues of legal disclosure? Confidentiality?

2. What models do you follow in your own keeping of confidences? What is at stake theologically?

3. What information does your judicatory provide on the legal issues related to clergy listening?

4. Do you know of anyone who has had legal difficulties in the area of disclosure of confidentialities? Describe.

5. Do you preface your counseling-listening with any comments about confidentiality and disclosure related to shared information? What do you say?

6. To whom would you first turn if either disclosure or confidentiality became an issue in your ministry?

7. What do your state laws say about disclosure of potentially harmful information heard in counseling?

*Five*

# Listening at Heart's Edge: God, Self, and Community

[The] process of birth [is] closely linked to the readiness to sustain a loss or an interior laceration. . . . And the activity of listening also involves an unavoidable process of mourning, which is the prelude to incipient processes of knowledge.
—Gemma Corradi Fiumara, *The Other Side of Language*

The type of listening discussed in this chapter has its roots in the contemplative tradition. "Contemplative" as used here means listening in relationship to the God/human dialogue as it is experienced both personally and corporately. It will also be termed "Godward listening." Elements of our pastoral listening definition understand this type of contemplative listening as "a theological activity, emerging from vocational and faith identity . . . [and which] can occur at sensory and non-sensory levels and is both individual and corporate in nature." The pastoral listener needs to ask: What does the minister's listening dialogue with God mean for self and others?

This chapter will explore the question through a combination of traditional and contemporary ideas about listening, beginning with a sampling of three influential, traditional approaches to listening from the early centuries of the Christian church to the present. Second, contemplative listening will be viewed through the Wolvin-Coakley taxonomy. Next, such listening will be explored through the use of "discernment" in the lives of ministers and their faith communities. In conclusion, excerpts from a paper on guided imagery will demonstrate how contemplative listening instruction and involvement can be extended into a faith community through the homiletical work of one parish pastor.

# Contemplative Listening: Strands of the Heritage

Various theologies over the centuries have mentioned listening, but few have actually applied it to faith and life, because listening has been tied to a complex of other ideas, dynamics, and concepts. The following three theologians provide a sample of some of the most influential writings on listening.

## The Rule of St. Benedict

Benedict's work provided the foundation of many later developments in the Christian contemplative tradition. Throughout his writings, he discusses silence, listening, speech, and the problems and obstacles in listening to God in community. The Rule's opening prologue begins: "Listen carefully, my son, to the master's instructions, and attend to them with the ear of the heart."[1]

The Rule places significant emphasis on the role of the pastoral leader, the abbot. He is the one who bears the main responsibility as chief listener in the community. He listens, monitors, and disciplines the listening of others and, when necessary, makes changes in the community through prayer and conversation to encourage all the community's participants to listen appropriately. The abbot is responsible for quelling the problems associated with four different types of non-listeners in the community: the "gyrating," "grumbling," "laughing," and "talking."[2] A Bible verse repeated in several places in reference to the abbot is: "Whoever listens to you, listens to me" (Luke 10:16). Thus, monastic obedience and listening are inseparable. "Speaking and teaching are the master's task; the disciple is to be silent and listen."[3]

Another listening discipline that The Rule enjoins is listening to the Word of God, accomplished by silence and through *lectio,* that is, the actual reading of the text:

> The formula of *lectio* is deceptively simple: read, meditate, pray, contemplate. But it assumes first and foremost a listening heart so that the routing is ensured and so that our journey to contemplation is not detoured. The sign that genuine listening takes place is that we bear fruit by being "words" or sacraments or signs to others, speaking the word to a noisy world in need of experiencing the power of the living word of God.[4]

*The Rule of St. Benedict* emphasizes listening as both individual and corporate. Listening and verbal repetition help form community life and ensure spiritual well-being. Benedict not only lays out scriptural passages to be read over the liturgical year; he also insists on the recitation of the Lord's Prayer "for all to hear, because thorns of contention are likely to spring up."[5] Readings from the church's theologians and the repeated reading of The Rule itself, recognizing the constant influx of new brothers, all demanded a daylong "ear of the heart." Benedict's Rule has had a major impact on monastic orders and in the ways Christians have listened in community over the centuries.

## Søren Kierkegaard

Another theologian engaged in matters of pastoral leadership, community, and listening is the nineteenth-century Danish writer Søren Kierkegaard. References to listening are scattered throughout his works. One of the most significant sections on listening appears in *Purity of Heart Is to Will One Thing,* the first in the series of *Edifying Addresses.*[6] Kierkegaard's emphasis in this work, intended as a preparation for confession, is on the relationship between the individual and God. Kierkegaard continually addresses the reader as "my listener" rather than "my reader." Section twelve, "What Must I Do? The Listener's Role in a Devotional Address," deals most specifically with listening.[7] As Kierkegaard discusses how a penitent listens to a spiritual address on confession read aloud, perhaps nowhere is the intricate listening dialogue between God and human more carefully explored. "In a devotional sense, earnestness: to listen in order to act, this is the highest thing of all, and, God be praised, every man is capable of it if he so wills."[8]

Kierkegaard describes the roles of the speaker of the devotional address, the penitent listener, and God as similar to a theater production. Like the spoken *lectio* named in *The Rule of St. Benedict,* silence, listening, contemplation, and speaking are all intertwined.

> But the speaker [of the address to the penitent] is not the actor— not in the remotest sense. No, the speaker is the prompter. There are no mere theatergoers present, for each listener will be looking into his own heart. The stage is eternity, and the listener, if he is the true listener (and if he is not, he is at fault) stands before God during the talk.[9]

As is typical of Kierkegaard's theology, he is rigorous in his focus on individual faith and on the responsibility of the believer for Godward listening.

## The Quaker Tradition: Douglas V. Steere

The American twentieth-century Quaker Douglas V. Steere has produced a major classic, *On Listening to Another,* which provides a phenomenology of listening for the Christian.[10] He offers this definition of a real listener:

> In order to listen discerningly to another, a certain maturity is required, a certain self-transcendence, a certain expectation, a patience, an openness to the new. In order to really listen, there must be a capacity to hear through many wrappings and only a mature listener, listening beyond the outer layer of the words that are spoken, is capable of this. (4)

Steere describes the good listener as one who meets the "spectator listener," who is the "listener within every speaker that listens while he speaks" (6). It is this spectator listener who assesses, challenges, and recognizes the true listener in any encounter to offer what Steere calls "acceptance, expectancy and constancy" (11). All of these characteristics exist in a more significant way in the presence of the "Eternal Listener," of God. Steere claims that only in listening to

> the hidden presence, the patient, all-penetrating Listener, the third member of every conversation whose existence, if not ignored, rebukes and damps down the evil and calls out and underlines the good, drawing from the invisible participants, things they did not know they possessed. (25)

The presence of this Listener actually defines the best of human listening: "a preciously thin membrane where the human and divine can be felt to mingle with the least opaque cloud of concealment [when] . . . the living Listener's presence may almost imperceptibly rise into awareness and with that awareness the total situation is altered" (27).

Steere's attention to listening focuses on community as a whole. He asks whether "all exercises of worship, all vocal ministry . . . serve to bring the worshippers into a corporate attentive awareness of the Living

Listener" (30). He describes Quaker worship forms that engage in listening and "vocal ministry," expressions of vocation in word and deed. Some of his insights regarding the relationship between word and silence will be discussed in the final chapter on constructing a theology of listening.

## Contemplative Listening with Wolvin-Coakley

The Wolvin-Coakley listening typology of discriminative, comprehensive, critical, therapeutic, and appreciative listening is reconfigured in different ways when applied to this aspect of good pastoral listening. The dialogue of listening among God, creature, and community operates at levels inclusive of, but beyond, the sensory. Such listening at a primary level is strictly interior, although God's actions in daily life are obviously "heard" through auditory/visual channels at all levels in an ongoing way. Listening undertaken with an implied Christian perspective is *incarnational listening*.

According to the principal definition of pastoral listening, good listening from the contemplative perspective resides with the inner life of the listener—whether lay or ordained. The stability, effectiveness, and safety of the listening context for the speaker are dependent wholly on this faith foundation, this relationship of listening to God demonstrated by the minister. However, lest listening be reduced to the idiosyncratic shape of the listener's emotional responses alone, it is important to remember that listening is also a theological activity. This entails a framing of reality that extends into the community in ways that are commonly understood and shared. They order—or disorder—the community's relationships with one another.

Applying the Wolvin-Coakley typology, discriminative listening, "listening to distinguish auditory and/or visual stimuli," does not apply to incarnational listening in the usual manner, except in the sense of dismissing or blocking out those stimuli that interfere with prayer and meditation.[11] Incarnational listening happens at a metaphorical rather than at a concrete level, as evidenced by biblical efforts to describe God's passages in daily life: "The wind blows where it chooses, and you hear the sound of it, but you do not know where it comes from or where it goes. So it is with everyone who is born of the Spirit" (John 3:8).

Likewise, "therapeutic" listening or "listening to a troubled sender" (see John 3:8) takes on a different nature. The human listener to God does not listen "therapeutically" in the sense of God as "troubled," although therapeutic listening may apply in the sense that God's troubled judgments against sinful activity are rendered in some form to the obedient listener. There can be, however, what I would term a "therapeutic listening expectation" in the person who seeks God's forgiveness and assistance. The other parts of the typology, the comprehensive, critical, and appreciative forms of listening, are generally employed at an interior level.

## What about Discernment?

*Discernment* is a word that is receiving new attention in contemporary theology. It certainly involves listening—in particular, Godward listening. The word is traditionally associated with human efforts to understand the movements of the spirit(s) that occur in seeking to know God and God's will; in the Bible it often refers to discovering the differences between good and evil spirits. It also used to describe the unfolding process of spiritual direction between a director and seeker.

What exactly is discernment? An intellectual capacity? A spiritual sense? A capacity for differentiation? A gift? The measure of one's vocation? The ability to distinguish sounds? The word has been used to mean all of this and more. With increased Protestant discussion and usage of the word, the term continues to gain more exposure and discussion. In the interests of an expanded use of this word, there are additional questions to consider: What are its sources and media of expression? Is it characteristic of individual or community activities? How is discernment understood in the context of one's own denominational history? What role does discernment play in pastoral ministry outside specific settings of spiritual direction?

Webster's defines discernment in relationship to "discern." The word comes from the Latin *discernere,* meaning to "separate, distinguish between." The definitions are in some sense contradictory: "1a: to detect with the eyes b: to detect with other senses than vision 2: to come to know or recognize mentally 3: to recognize or identify as separate and distinct."[12] In other words, discernment is variously sensory or nonsensory and mental in nature. Thornton offers this definition of spiritual discernment:

a general ability to understand and interpret a person's spiritual
state and religious experience. . . . this may be a charismatic gift
(1 Cor 12:10) or a skill acquired by experience, or some combination of both. Discernment of spirits . . . is a much more complex
and technical process based upon a profound ascetical theology
. . . and expanded throughout the ages by the Desert Fathers.[13]

Another definition not included in Thornton's has to do with corporate
Pauline theology related to the Eucharist. In his discussions with the
Corinthians, Paul tells them that "For all who eat and drink without
discerning the body, eat and drink judgment against themselves"
(1 Cor 11:29).

Further complicating the history of discernment is its relative
absence in pastoral care literature. Why is this? Using Thornton's two
definitions, pastoral use of discernment in faith communities is rare
except in the Roman Catholic tradition of spiritual direction and in
certain charismatic parts of the Christian tradition. This leaves a
descriptive gap in speaking about how ministers listen to themselves
and others in the course of their daily work. Their listening is clearly
not passive nor simply based on good secular listening skills. What
accounts for this gap? There are several possible explanations.

First, in traditions that do not instruct leaders theologically and
specifically in terms of the fruit and gifts of the Spirit, there may be
ignorance or confusion about what discernment is. Its use has also
been confined to relationships that are individual rather than corporate
in nature, such as counseling or spiritual direction: almost no literature
exists on corporate discernment. What does it mean for a group of
people to engage in the process of discernment in a spiritual, rather
than in a strictly problem-solving, sense? What happens to a community, to its power structures, and to its individual members when a
minister and a faith community embark upon group discernment? The
new dean of a seminary raised these same questions in a recent installation address:

Perhaps more than ever, we as primarily a Christian faith community need to be disciplined in corporate discernment, and
with regularity and intentionality bring our multiple selves into
conversation with one another, so that when we speak and act as
a school of theological education, we do so prayerfully, from our

corporate Christian heart and soul. . . . We can do this by remembering to regularly ask together: What is going on here? What are we doing? Is it faithful? And, what are we called to be here and now? Seeking to notice God's leading presence in the midst of our multiplicity, we can be unafraid to reexamine, reorganize, reshape, and even re-vision.[14]

Some forms of guidance in discernment are sought by groups, although they are generally separate and specific in relation to the rest of the group's discussions. For example, a prayer for guidance or a meditation may be offered at the beginning of a church council meeting. But what of discernment as a permeable dynamic operating throughout group discussion and action?

Another issue, often unacknowledged, has to do with the use of pastoral power. Depending on the power structures of a faith community, pastoral leadership may express disinterest in allowing the corporate process of discernment to unfold, since it would jeopardize traditional notions of leaders and followers. What if pastoral leadership encourages corporate discernment but chooses to be exempt from the process? This makes discernment an issue for those who have "a problem" and the responsibility of those seeking enlightenment. To some extent, the spiritual arrogance of the minister involved defeats the efforts of the group. Contemplative listening is foundational, the baseline form of listening, which controls and affects all other types of pastoral listening. In its absence, pastoral leadership falters and fails. In a nineteenth-century article on the validity of the preacher's word, the author acerbically notes, "The very worst thing that can happen to a congregation and its office is the fiery, seemingly ascetic, deeply prayerful zeal of a preacher, who has carried many to repentance, who has shown at last the goat's foot, or from whom the mask will some time fall off, because a bad tree brings forth bad fruit."[15]

In keeping with our original assertion that the kind of listening we are talking about is corporate, parishioners are influenced and formed by the minister's listening, whatever types of Godward listening they do. Listening is a form of witness, of testimony! As a template for other types of congregational listening, the omnipresent background of the pastoral/godly relationship will invoke corporate critical listening. According to the Wolvin-Coakley typology, this category elicits responses about [pastoral] ethos—its credibility and viability. I am hopeful that corporate critical listening can evoke deeper appreciative listening as well.

If discernment should be a part of personal and community faith, life, and work, what is the connection between it and listening that occurs in all pastoral contexts? It seems that the reasons for the ignorance or avoidance of discernment reside not only in denominational history, but also in the lack of listening instruction, and in challenges to power structures produced by a view of the church that values corporate discernment and shifting definitions of discernment. This latter seems particularly true as both the Protestant and Roman Catholic traditions of pastoral care appear to be moving toward one another in new ways.[16]

Written spiritual resources reflect another element of pastoral Godward listening. Most faith traditions have some structured verbal or written daily form of Godward listening in place, whether that is the breviary, reading the Bible, or following the daily forms set out in Luther's catechism.[17] If Godward pastoral listening—that is, the personal faith relationship of the minister—is "overheard" in faith communities, it would seem that a logical response would be for the pastor to connect with parishioners through different instructional methods of Godward listening to deepen the mutuality of discernment. An experiment in this direction follows.

## Corporate Forms of Listening: Invitation to Faith

A unique form of instructing congregational members in Godward listening in worship was developed in a paper on guided imagery by a Gettysburg class participant.[18] He used the guided imagery technique for his proclamation at an Easter sunrise service. The following excerpts describe the pastor's attempt to cultivate Godward listening in his people through congregational involvement in proclamation in a new way on Easter.

> *When most people hear the term "imagery," they immediately think it means something strictly visual. However, when I refer to imagery for this project, I am using the definition of the trained professionals in this area: "any perception that comes through any of the senses. That means sights, sounds, smells, tastes, and feel."*

*Guided imagery involves listening on a verbal and nonverbal level both by the leader and by the participant. To be effective the use of guided imagery encourages sharing between the listener and the speaker. . . . The listener is affected by such key variables as the environment (that is, temperature, lighting, noise levels); hemispheric specialization (oftentimes the use of the right side of the brain); physical and psychological states, attitudes, self-concepts; receiver apprehensions; time, listener preferences, feedback, and a personal sense of the influence of key variables at any point in his/her listening.*

*This leads to the first operating principle of imagery, "Our bodies don't discriminate between sensory images in the mind and what we call reality." The second key principal . . . "In this altered state [induced by the imagery], we are capable of more rapid and intense healing, growth, learning, and change." . . . The third principle that operates with guided imagery and its effectiveness is that it is "something that is entirely within our control, for use when, how, and where we want it."*

*There are at least eight distinct types of imagery: feeling-state, end-state, cellular, physiological, metaphoric, energetic, psychological, and spiritual. . . . imagery . . . elicits your sense of communion with the Divine. It is imagery that aims directly with connection with God, or for an opening into a larger world that extends beyond our concrete everyday reality.*

*Guided imagery involves "comprehensive listening skills" as it increases our concentration and, over time through repetition, becomes imbedded in our long-term memories. Another example of the utilization of "comprehensive listening skills" is in choosing the right atmosphere. The use of guided imagery [also] involves "therapeutic listening skills." For example, empathy is involved, which is defined as feeling and thinking with another person. To effectively develop guided imagery we must listen to a person, learn about his or her thoughts, life experiences, joys, sorrows, aches, pains, symptoms, etc.*

*Using your voice and pacing yourself involves "discriminative listening skills," while observing verbal and nonverbal cues within the setting. The leader is to speak in a calm, comforting, and steady manner. The voice should flow. As the guided meditation progresses and as the participants' awareness increases, the leader may begin speaking more softly. As a person relaxes, hearing acuity increases. The voice crescendos when suggesting tension and decrescendos when suggesting relaxation. Near the end of the guided meditation, the voice is at an easily heard volume.*

"Critical listening is listening to comprehend and then evaluate the message." When listening to guided imagery, the listener needs to accept or reject a message on the basis of sound criteria. Is the person leading the guided imagery credible and trustworthy? Does it go along with my ethics and values? Is it helpful or harmful? For listening should be critical especially when the listener is exposed to a persuasive message—a message designed to influence a change in the listener. Workshops are becoming more limited to those with a credible background who would use it ethically.

[At the Easter sunrise service] my sermon was entitled "An Easter Reflection." The sermon gave the congregation the opportunity to journey to the tomb, to be part of the Easter story, and, like Mary Magdalene, to meet the risen Savior who offers and gives new life. I briefly explained to the congregation about the concept of guided imagery and then stated the guidelines. I invited the congregation to close their eyes and breathe deeply. As they journeyed to the open tomb I assured them, unlike the women in the story, they had nothing to fear, for we know that the Savior is alive. Through guided imagery, the people could experience the sights, sounds, smells, and the feeling of the earth beneath their feet while on their journey.

After the service, one person told me she appreciated the journey . . . [since] when she was in the Holy Land a few years ago she was very disappointed . . . because of the commercialism. All this cheapened the whole experience with irreverence toward the gospel. Experiencing the Easter message [one man said] was intriguing as he felt so focused and that the rest of the congregation was so focused as they listened to the sermon. He didn't know what caused him to listen in a new way. It was a positive, reenergizing experience for him.

Throughout the guided imagery, I was listening for both verbal and nonverbal responses. I was looking forward to feedback afterward. It opened up communication with other people and we could dialogue about the sermon and the impact of listening on their life experience.

## Summary

As a component of good pastoral listening, Godward listening is rooted in the contemplative traditions of the church, expressing the deepest elements of personal and vocational faith and action. Such listening has ramifications for the web of personal and corporate relationships in any faith community. According to Wolvin-Coakley's typology, it utilizes all levels of listening but differs from them in some unique ways.

Effective pastoral ministry always seeks to prompt instruction and sharing in Godward listening and discernment. Of all the listening unique to the Christian faith, pastoral listening must have Godward listening as its baseline; without it other forms of listening are rendered ineffective or insincere.

## For Discussion

1. How do you listen for God? What models do you use in your listening?

2. What parts of the contemplative tradition have influenced your listening? Are these from your own or from other faith traditions?

3. How would you evaluate the contemplative listening skills of your current faith community?

4. What is already in place in your faith community that encourages and teaches people how to listen to God and to one another? Are these in written, verbal, or kinetic forms?

5. How do you define discernment?

6. How does your current faith community practice corporate discernment?

7. What connection do you see between proclamation in the traditional sense and the use of guided imagery as sermon?

8. What stumbling blocks do you and others encounter in listening to God?

*Six*

# Corporate Godward Listening: Worship and Preaching

"Lord, hear my voice!
Let your ears be attentive
 to the voice of my supplications!"
—PSALM 130:2

"And how are they to hear without someone to proclaim him?"
—ROMANS 10:14b

Regardless of the listening contexts present in any faith community, it is in the worship setting that the pastoral leader is most challenged by the simultaneous, multilayered demands made on her or his listening skills. Worship is a profoundly long-term interactive event, regardless of the speech or silence that patterns it, because worship has consequences that follow its weekly advent. The pastoral leadership listening essential for worship is addressed first in this chapter by looking at worship planning and its components. Next, preaching, though an integral part of worship, is discussed in relationship to the reciprocal acts of listening involved.

## Listening in Worship

Every aspect of the definition of pastoral listening given earlier is included in the worship leadership role, which will be examined using the Wolvin-Coakley taxonomy. We will also look at nonverbal codes of behavior and "schema theory." The primary focus here, as in other parts of this book, will be on the structures of listening, although the contents, the "listening for," will also be discussed.

Listening in worship presents an ever-shifting array of the listening categories noted in Wolvin-Coakley: comprehensive, discriminative, critical, therapeutic, and appreciative. Knowledge of these types serves as a useful tool in worship planning. These types may work together to form a coherent worship service or be counterproductive in one another's company.

While listeners may be unaware they are even listening in these various ways, leaders can use the categories as a grid to examine the relevance, congruency, and effectiveness of coherent worship services. For example, on a Sunday when the biblical texts speak strongly to harsh issues of judgment and accountability, the texts will clash with preaching, which is heard generally (as well as specifically) as therapeutic. The dissonance will be "heard" at several levels. A worship service that asks the listeners to attend to worship without attempting to elicit the appreciative listening response will result in an aesthetically displeasing experience for some listeners.

It is impossible to privilege one type of listening over another in worship planning, nor should there be any reason to do so given the range of naturally preferred or chosen modes of hearing. There are exceptions when major celebrations or tragedies determine the predominant mode of listening for a majority of the worshipers; for example, a funeral service may be heard in the therapeutic mode. Planners have some control over individual and corporate attentiveness, but congregations fluctuate in mood from week to week and so do the many variables that affect worship.

There are usually consistent listening patterns and forms, however, which provide stabilizing factors in enabling the worshiper to listen well: the lectionary, the seasons of the church year, the repetition of ritual, hearing the same voices—literally—in worship leadership, the visual presence of the same objects and persons week after week.

Listening in worship involves an entire congregation and its worship leaders. The quality of the worship event is in direct ratio to the attentive listening given it by the minister. Where does this start? A useful approach in worship planning is to ask questions about its meanings and functions from the perspective of listening. Those seated on worship committees, pastoral leadership, and musicians need to ask: How are we listening in worship? What and who is it that we want worshipers to hear? To listen to? The questions are not as easily answered as one might think. Such questions, if we dare to ask them, are significantly ecclesial-political in nature; decisions to change worship may have serious ramifications.

## Three Listening Factors in Worship

Three listening issues need attention from worship planners in order to set the stage for worship. One is the use of equipment and furniture to enhance listening in the worship space; the second is the role of silence in worship; and the third—a combination of the first two—is producing auditory and visual messages that do not consistently contradict one another. This latter statement reflects the Wolvin-Coakley definition of listening, which emphasizes the role that the visual plays in listening.

Worship planners need to start with the basics of discriminative listening. Does the public address system (if there is one) suit the majority of listeners? Are those with hearing problems offered any type of listening assistance? Public address systems also need to be tuned appropriately for male and female voice levels and volume. Another perennial question, auditory and political in nature, includes: Why do numbers of worshipers choose to sit in the rear of the church (and often complain of being unable to hear)? Are changes in seating and chancel arrangements —sometimes very long-term projects—a good way to tackle less obvious theological issues?

Along with chancel renovation and pew rearrangement, one parish sent encouraging monthly pastoral letters explaining the liturgical and historical reasons for the modifications. This necessary change in worship listening habits did not come quickly or easily.

One of the most problematic aspects of worship planning, including those moments of preparation prior to worship itself, raises the issue of the role of silence as a context for listening. Is the given worship community comfortable with silence, engaging in it at particular times during worship? Do the rubrics of the printed liturgy specify silence? Are these directions actually followed? Is time allowed prior to worship, without other distractions, to encourage people to prepare for worship? How knowledgeable and comfortable are worship leaders themselves with silence? The "sounds of silence" present a direct challenge to pastoral leaders. If needed, worship leaders should decide how to begin the educational process for the entire congregation, helping members learn to be at ease with silence.

In some parishes, silence before worship—indicating a receptivity to God's presence prior to worship—is not valued or deemed necessary. Instead, conversation before worship with other members or worship leaders is encouraged as a way to build community. Pastoral leadership must decide which of these is most important or how they can be balanced. In other settings, the musical prelude either encourages conversation or signals the actual beginning of the worship service. The question about silence in worship is also important to ask in terms of what is not being said and what needs to be voiced, which could be the silence produced by lack of lay voices, female voices, ethnic voices, children's voices. Perhaps issues need "speaking," such as those related to injustice, inactivity, and denial.

Finally, it is important that visual factors in the place of worship do not conflict with what is heard. Some of the many visual distractions that can inhibit good listening include: leading worship in front of brightly lit stained glass windows (producing an effect called halation); using vestments and liturgical items that are too dramatic or too small in proportion to the rest of the sanctuary; improper use of lighting; pulpit and lecterns that are too small or large for the readers and preachers; and chancel furniture that is placed inappropriately.

## Nonverbal Codes of Behavior

Many types of sensory stimuli play a key role in prompting interest or distracting the faith community from listening in worship. How worship planners address these plays an important function in determining the viability of worship as a means of enhancing or disrupting community. Several major areas of nonverbal human behavior determine how people listen and are specified in these three types of codes: (1) visual and auditory: kinesics, physical appearance, and vocalics; (2) contact codes: haptics and proxemics; (3) place and time codes: environment, artifacts, and chronemics.[1] All of these come into play in the worship setting and often provide a subtle but powerful background influence. Kinesics is defined as "the Greek word for 'movement' and refers to all forms of body movement, excluding physical contact with another's body. "The popular expression *body language* is almost exclusively concerned with this code."[2] Physical appearance is represented across a spectrum as wide as that of humanity. Communication experts have catalogued numerous examples of the impact appearances play in listening, and it is this code that contains the widest number and range of non-verbal signifiers. Most forms of worship, liturgical or not, employ ritual items, attire, gestures, and actions. "Vocalics" can be described as the enactment of the voice's possibilities, apart from actually speaking words. Examples of vocalics are pace, pitch, volume, inflection, dialect, timbre, resonance, and range.

The second category includes "haptics," which is the "perception and use of touch as communication," and "proxemics," which is the "perception, use, and structuring of *space* as communication."[3] It is easy to see how these contact codes can enrich and complicate worship, since they are possessed of "[n]onverbal situational features [that] can affect communication by setting expectations for interaction, prompting the use of different social rules, and clarifying roles for interaction."[4]

The third and final category, "chronemics," involves environment and time, "how humans perceive, structure, and use time as communication."[5] This issue may be hotly debated in many parishes by those who understand worship as occurring in one hour ("think of the parking problems for the next service") and those who wish worship time to extend itself in a more "kairotic" sense, concluding "when it's over."

Worship planners should use these codes as effective ways of prompting listening without losing themselves in details that promote contradictions. For example, if worship proceeds with a demand for listening receptivity through silence and contradicts that with visual messages—such as liturgical ministers who do not know their roles or nonverbal behavior on the part of worship leaders uncomfortable with silence—worshipers' listening attempts will be hampered. Listening and visual cues must reinforce each other appropriately.

What if a new minister decides to lead a more informal style of worship (unannounced) than the congregation is accustomed to? He touches the people periodically with a handshake or hug, decides against wearing the usual liturgical garb of his denomination, and preaches and leads worship in an informal and humorous tone of voice. In retrospect, the minister's interpretation of the congregation's distaste for this service should not be immediately dismissed as the members' inability to engage in community or hear the gospel. The minister has obviously disregarded certain habits of haptics, proxemics, and vocalics that typify this parish's normal life.

It is difficult to say which of these codes may be violated the most frequently as ministers and people miss listening to one another through worship. Certainly the most publicized of the codes has to do with haptics—with touch. Ministers, congregations, and judicatories face responses to touch ranging from acceptance to reluctance to charges of sexual molestation. The use of touch has its roots in biblical practices and is properly expressed in both sacramental and non-sacramental ways in church: "exchanging the peace" is one example.[6] Haptics can contribute to parish and personal life in a variety of ways. This nonverbal element of listening should be thoroughly understood by the minister and worship planners in all its negative and positive dimensions.[7]

## Listening in Worship: Schema Theory

While the Wolvin-Coakley taxonomy demonstrates the types of listening that can occur during worship, there is another way to describe the process of how we pattern the types of listening employed. One useful way to consider the listening of all worship participants is through "schema theory" from the field of cognitive psychology. The theory addresses the ways we think about what we hear and how we interpret information. What this means for listening is that we first receive information through earlier information grids we have already established mentally. "These schemata relate persons or objects to attributes or relate actions to anticipated consequences."[8]

The schemata serve several functions for arranging information:

1. Schemata tell us to what we should attend.

2. Schemata serve as a framework for interpreting incoming information.

3. Schemata guide the reconstruction of messages in memory.[9]

If this theory is applied to the rhythms of community, weekly Sunday worship, and liturgical participation, the schemata are particularly useful to understanding listening in worship. In other words, the listener / worshiper comes with a set of specific and high expectations about what he or she will encounter in the worship; the liturgy or conduct of the service follows a certain pattern and tends to be heavily scripted through the accumulation of history and tradition. For the worship leader, then, there are already many "givens" in worship. This can be either a positive or a negative, depending on what the worship leaders are proposing.

"Telling us to what we should attend" means worship planners that offer poorly planned, disjointed, or inappropriate liturgy—or worship formats that are radically separated from the traditions and history of the faith community—will only confuse the listener; actually, they will produce a non-listener.

Schemata, in telling us what to attend to, means that worship planners should also take into account the significant role of several different types of repetition used in worship. The use of repetition in liturgical and preaching formulas is typical of most faith traditions. Repetition is an expected and anticipated part of worship. In fact, repetition fulfills all three aspects of the schema theory well. The study of repetitive speech is a special branch of communication; the value of repetitive speech cannot be overestimated. Some types of repetition that worshipers hear and listen for are:

> A full repetition is an utterance that replicates all of a previous utterance. A partial repetition is an utterance that replicates only part of an earlier repetition. A literal repetition is an utterance that replicates the words of a previous utterance, regardless of the words. A spontaneous repetition is one that arises from a speaker's own initiative based on his or her judgment of a prevailing situation. An obligatory repetition is one that a speaker is required to utter by regulation or convention. An effective repetition is one that succeeds in having the impact on the hearer that the speaker intends it to have.[10]

That schemata is "a framework for interpreting incoming information" suggests that there are always possibilities for growth and change within worship as long as it does not deviate radically or generally from congregational listeners' former experiences. Well-planned worship can act as a bridge to lead the faithful to new places of insight and spiritual depth.

The most exciting proposal for worship listening, however, has to do with the third point in the schemata. "Reconstruction" does not just mean repetition; it also refers to a reconfiguring of former memories in the service of the present and the future. A recent cereal advertisement captures this point perfectly: "Taste it again for the first time!"[11] The concept of memory reconstruction is directly linked to "anamnesis," remembering what the celebration of the Eucharist declares—that the Christ remembered is the one who, by the worshipers' remembrance, recreates the present. This re-creative, remembering dynamic is precisely what gives meaning to other faith realities such as repentance, forgiveness, and God's active grace.

Obviously, worship listeners may have consistently exercised poor worship habits or are in ignorance of a number of elements of the faith life. Complicating this is the fact that sinful human beings, who compose worshiping assemblies, are often resistant to the gospel's call to repentance. They may wish not to attend to, reconstruct, or remember painful or problematic realities when encountering the gospel's persuasiveness and its call to listen differently to life. In other words, there can be spiritual issues working at cross-purposes in the schemata of the listeners. All of these can affect how they listen and the channels through which they process information.

Nevertheless, the schemata offer the minister-listener a framework by which to understand and evaluate a congregation's listeners for worship planning, reiterate core faith priorities through more than merely incantational repetition, locate areas of the faith that demand more emphasis in Christian education, or offer as-yet unheard elements of the gospel to the listeners.

## Preaching: Listening to the Listener

Although good preaching—preaching worth hearing—is an integral part of worship, its nature demands a separate analysis from overall worship planning. Nowhere is the act of listening in worship more focused, misunderstood, or parodied than the act of preaching. No other part of a worship service is subject to more public discussion than the singular act of proclamation. No other worship event requires the comprehensive and critical listening skills of the parishioners more than this one; all five types of basic listening are in full swing as the pew occupant lends an ear and the minister stands alone and speaks to the corporate body of Christ.

What then does it mean to listen to preaching as a pastoral leader? Such listening entails several things. It includes a lifelong commitment to listening constantly to the lives of the faithful, listening for God, and listening to the self as preacher. Listening to a sermon is a fiercely reciprocal, intense activity. It begins with the listening the preacher does in sermon preparation. As in worship planning, the preacher begins listening long before entering the pulpit. The texts, the season, the preacher's individual choice of sermonic direction help focus the sermon, always with the parish as a participant in that process. This, then, is followed by the listening both preacher and people do during the event of proclamation and what the preacher hears as a result of that preaching in the days ahead. It means listening in the aftermath in such a way that the information is turned into more attentive preaching. Sermons express the fullness and effectiveness of the preacher's listening habits.

This chapter will not "type" listeners or decide which sermonic forms best suit them. At best, that is a provisional exercise. The decision about sermonic forms is really more a matter of faith and trust in the gospel's power, since a sermon for a community cannot be designed with only an individual listener in mind. As Long notes, "The gospel comes to us in a wide variety of forms, and the preacher who faithfully bears witness [listens to] the gospel will allow the fullness of the gospel to summon forth a rich diversity of sermon forms, as well."[12] More to our purposes is the examination of how the preacher listens to the act of preaching, given the forms of listening and processing information that she or he and all parishioners share.

Fortunately, for the minister committed to improving listening skills in proclamation, interest in listening to the listener has increased in the field of homiletical communication over the past decade. For much of Christianity's proclamatory history, two foci have formed what people hear in preaching. First, the rhetoric of the faith has traditionally emphasized the importance of the Bible and scriptural truths, the Word, regardless of the state or condition of the listeners. Christian truth was generally considered to be self-evident and the listener was confronted with a sermonic "take it or leave it" attitude.

Additionally, the role of the speaker has figured largely in centuries-long debates over the role of ethos in persuasion. The nineteenth-century Phillips Brooks dictum still reigns in many pulpits: "Preaching . . . has in it two essential elements, truth and personality."[13] Other than an obligatory nod to Paul's statements on listening to the preacher, most manuals on preaching say little or nothing about the functions listening and the listener prompt in relationship to preaching.

Analyzing the pew occupants' homiletical listening habits is necessary and helpful for today's preachers. It can save both preachers and listeners from the severest forms of irrelevancy and unbelief. It has also taken on a critical urgency with the acknowledged shortcomings of monologuist forms of address in an age of interactive media. Listening more intensely is demanded by newly emerging interpretations of pastoral leadership and power, the advantages of sermonic participation by the laity (witness preaching in the black tradition), and the increased tendency of worshipers to find a preacher who suits their needs and proclivities.

Despite the proclaimer's best efforts to listen to the people, what does it mean if the people are choosing not to listen? Certainly, the preacher's role as "prophet" may come to the fore. The prophetic preaching tradition varies in intensity and meaning from one faith perspective to another. There are also other issues related to the inability to listen/hear that will be discussed in chapter 7.

## A Homiletical Listening History

The history of the listening preacher is sketchy at best. No theologian has written a treatise on the contours of homiletical listening from the perspective of the pastoral leader.[14] The following sample of theological thinking on this issue provides some interesting insights into the acknowledged connections between listening and preaching. In the first homiletical manual of the western church, Augustine asks the speaker to become a listener-preacher: "He who seeks to teach in speech what is good, spurning none of these things, that is, to teach, to delight, and to persuade, *should pray and strive that he be heard intelligently, willingly, and obediently.*"[15]

One of the pithiest examples of what is at stake in listening was included in a sermon on the Gospel of John by Martin Luther. In a sermonic dialogical vignette, Luther says:

Well, so far as I am concerned, you need not mend your ways. I shall not yield, and you will not yield. But on the Day of Judgment God will ask me: "Did you preach that?" and I will be able to say yes. Then he will turn to you with the question: "Did you hear that sermon?" And you will answer yes. And in reply to God's next question to you: "Why, then, did you not believe it?" you will say: "Oh, I took it to be the mere word of man, spoken by a poor chaplain or village pastor!" And now this Word, implanted in your heart, will accuse you and be your accuser and judge on the Last Day.[16]

Fred Craddock, one of the twentieth century's great homileticians, urged the preacher's closer attention to listening in his book, *Overhearing the Gospel: Preaching and Teaching the Faith to Persons Who Have Heard It All Before.*[17] In the chapter entitled "The Experience of the Listener," Craddock dialogues with the perspectives of the Danish theologian Søren Kierkegaard (see chapter 5). He discusses the "overhearing" of the gospel represented in Kierkegaard's works. While the concept of over-hearing is only one element of what it means to listen multiphasically, Craddock's comments are worth further exploration. He notes that con-temporary trends in speech communication have been detrimental to listening:

> The encounter and confrontation models have come to dominate formal settings for communication. . . . In theological and bibli-cal circles, encounter achieved the status of a canon by which to evaluate the scholarly enterprise. . . . But even so, I do lament one serious loss. By defining the Word of God as address [alone], the experience of the hearer was contracted to a decision, an act of the will. The posture of confrontation gave no room for the happy accident of overhearing. "Once upon a time" capitulated to "once for all."[18]

Craddock's insights are part of his careful arguments for inductive preaching, hearing the everyday experiences of the listener in such a way as to craft more effective narrative sermons.

Another recent work, *Theology for Preaching: Authority, Truth, and Knowledge of God in a Postmodern Ethos,* contains a helpful essay by Ronald Allen, "Modes of Discourse for the Sermon in the Postmodern World."[19] It summarizes the preacher's work in assessing the listening capabilities of the congregation. Pastoral leaders should consider devel-oping a "listener profile"—using some of the resources reviewed in this chapter—to ensure better preaching. Many of the books listed may be located in bookstores under "congregational studies" or "psychology."

# Summary

The listening of a faith community is most obvious and complex during worship: all the five forms of listening by Wolvin-Coakley are in play. It is an interesting yet crucial lens for worship planning to ask how, why, where, and when people listen in worship. This includes attention to the visual, the nonverbal, and the role of silence. Since sensory stimuli of many types play a significant role in how people listen, worship planners and leaders must understand and coordinate these through the codes with which people process information: visual and auditory; contact codes; place and time codes.

Because people interpret what they listen to together with what they see, the use of schemata theory enables worship planners and leaders to create more in-depth worship. Schemata theory supports old forms of worship and demonstrates how to introduce new ones. In schemata theory, repetition plays a key role in reinforcing faith through what people hear, reiterate, remember, and hope for.

Homiletical literature has rarely discussed listening to preaching as a preacher and as a pew occupant. This is changing, however, partially because of a renewed interest in rhetoric and also because of a heightened appreciation of audience diversity. For better or for worse, the perceived quality of pastoral ethos determines to whom worshipers choose to listen. This latter issue can supercede any claims made by Scripture, tradition, or a faith community.

# For Discussion

1. According to the Wolvin-Coakley taxonomy, does worship in your local setting tend to function at one or two levels of listening more than others? If so, what is at stake for participants, theologically and personally, in keeping worship at only one or two levels?

2. How is silence factored into your church's worship? If it is, why? If not, why not?

3. Of the nonverbal codes, which are those that receive the most attention from worship planners? The least? Why?

4. Have any of these codes proven problematic in the congregation? Provide details to support your answer.

5. According to the definition of pastoral listening, which of the nonverbal codes seems most problematic in relationship to your worship tradition regarding "ecclesiastic settings and constraints?"

6. According to the schema theory, does your current faith community experience any significant problems in how they listen? (For example, how does one establish and repeat patterns of worship for new Christians?)

7. What do you understand as the role of repetition in preaching and worship?

8. What attention have you consciously given to listening as an ongoing homiletical project?

*Seven*

# "Where Two or Three Are Gathered": Listening in Groups

Listening is . . . a moral act. . . . an act of attending to the other that discloses the strangeness of otherness, disrupting our comfortable self-images and threatening to undo our everyday experiences of ourselves (and others). . . . Listeners are required not only to welcome the strangeness of the other but to risk self-disclosure in the act of listening.

—Lloyd Steffen, *The Christian Century*

The pastoral listener is constantly engaged in meetings of two or more individuals: committees, governing groups of the ministry setting or judicatory, ecumenical gatherings, community groups, ad hoc sessions. With the extension of technology, this can also include teleconferences and long-distance learning groups. Commissions, task forces, and loosely connected networks all have different constituencies, needs, and directions. Within them, each additional individual joining a group both complicates and enriches communications.

Since most of the institutional, organizational work of a faith community is carried out in these meetings, decision making regarding programs, human resources, and finances can intensify the need for certain types of listening. The fields of organizational communications, industrial psychology, and small group communications continue to produce and refine various theories about how people speak and listen in such settings.[1] Like so many seemingly simple transactions, this field of communications offers ideas and research that are open-ended, complex, and sometimes in dispute.

This chapter will discuss some useful basic terms and dynamics from these various fields and relate them to the pastoral leader as listener in these groups. According to our definition of pastoral listening, such settings require: "a command of listening skills and structures . . . subject to pertinent societal and ecclesiastical boundaries." It is also true that pastoral listening in these group situations challenges "the vocational and faith identity" of the minister-listener when conflict is part of the meeting. The Gettysburg Seminary pastors' class on listening disclosed that, indeed, these settings of multiple participants were the ones most fraught with difficulties and anxieties for them. One can readily sympathize with Jesus' own fretful complaint to his disciples: "Do you not yet understand?" (Mark 8:21).

The following elements of listening in group settings will be addressed: (1) the basic listening frameworks applying to a majority of meetings in faith communities; (2) communication guidelines for listening in meetings; (3) the role turn-taking plays in listening (an extension of the nonverbal codes); (4) the manifestations of listening levels in the Wolvin-Coakley listening grid as they can be applied to pastoral listening in groups; (5) insights from one pastor's attempts to listen to the participants in her staff meeting. Finally, from the Quaker tradition, a unique form of listening to others may offer a disciplined form of listening training for those working in groups.

## Faith Community Frameworks

Generally, faith communities have some rules in place for conducting meetings that provide the framework for the pastoral listener. Ignorance of the frames or illegitimate efforts to listen outside the frames will place interactions at a disadvantage. What are some of these frames? They may be implicit or explicit, formal or informal. A group's constitution or committee structure can all give shape to the listening context. The community's long-standing habits of listening to one another provide another constant frame. Many denominations use *Robert's Rules of Order*—not only for keeping order but also for doing the business of the denomination in a fashion that is legally accountable.[2]

A parish's mission statement, with any luck an indication of a community that has already listened to itself and to its mission, is another listening frame for groups meeting under its auspices. Many meetings have either a written or informal but regular agenda. If parishioners are unaware of any of these basic documents or verbal structures, the parish leader is responsible for introducing them in order to facilitate the ongoing mutual task of better listening. A parish leadership retreat at the beginning of the church year that— among other things—establishes and teaches procedures for listening, will be an invaluable tool for the future workings of the group.

Another fascinating frame that impacts group listening and one that has received cultural attention recently is that of the dynamic of "civility." What types of courtesies are expected from and understood by all the participants of any group's meetings? This question certainly has cultural, age, and gender connotations; it is one worth asking. Civility is also an issue of power and directly reflects the power structures in place among laity and clergy. Sadly, some structures force the majority of participants to be constant listeners with only minimal opportunities to respond. An "in your face'" form of meeting may be the cultural norm in some areas and could provide some shocks to a new clergy listener.

## Listening in Meetings

Regardless of faith perspectives, some general rules apply when listening in meetings. There are many different goals for which meetings are convened: exchanging ideas, creating solutions, engaging in argument for positive or negative reasons, allocating funding, settling conflicts. As a result, it is necessary to focus to some extent on the reciprocal nature of the listening/speaking process. This all requires the dynamic of active listening, which intends to

1. Create a supportive listening environment.
2. Keep the focus of the conversation on the other person[s].
3. Generate supportive nonverbal behavior, which requires conscious eye contact.
4. Value alternative experiences.[3]

Implicit in these descriptions of good listening are a number of issues related to the previously discussed nonverbal codes, of which eye contact is only one of many. The codes both emerge out of and generate listening in a mutually reciprocal way and have to do with a key question: How do people listen in meetings and how are ideas exchanged as a result? Communications theorists raise an interesting definition in relationship to what is heard/listened to: A *conversation* is a series of opportunities to speak and listen. It is made up of *turns*, when one speaker has sole possession of the floor. Order, length, and content of turns can all vary, depending on the occasion and participants.[4]

The research on conversational turns and turn-taking is complex; for example, the phrase "the conversation took a turn" suggests a variety of meanings. Researchers differ on matters of sequence, significance, and interpretations of turn-taking, particularly when gender is involved. However, there are a number of basic moves that people make in conversations as they speak and listen.

Speakers can give one of two categories of cues to those around them. These are "turn-suppressing cues" or "turn yielding cues."[5] Some examples of the first are speaking more loudly, looking away from the listener, or continuing a gesture. Examples of the second type of cues are making eye contact, lowering intonation, decreasing voice volume, or slowing the tempo of one's words.

Listeners can engage in three different types of cues in response to what they are hearing: first, they may show "turn-requesting cues," such as gazing directly at the speaker, nodding the head, or raising the index finger. A second category of turn cues is something called "backchannel cues." The listener will give these nonverbal cues without any desire to speak but rather to indicate responses (positive or negative) to what is being said. Some of these include changed facial expressions, nodding, and vocalics like groans or mumbles. The third category of cues from listeners is "turn-denying cues." Anyone who remembers trying to avoid the teacher's look in order to escape being called on has used these cues! They include looking away from the speaker, silence, or relaxed, disinterested body posture.[6]

On a more comprehensive level, the listening-speaking flow of conversation in meetings is governed by two approaches to subjects. The first is *episodes,* which are "periods within conversations when the discussion focuses on a particular topic."[7] Next there are *positions,* which are "segments of interaction within an episode in which a person maintains a consistent disposition toward the topic and other conversants."[8]

The listener can respond to the turn-taking across episodes and positions (topic management) with a range of emotions and nonverbal behavior. A listener can employ four types of nonverbal boundary markers for these purposes. The first is through *proxemic* (use of personal space) shifts, which are changes in leaning backward or forward. These can signify changes in either episodes or positions. Another is *extrainteractional activities*. Examples of this nonverbal behavior include standing up (if seated), pulling down a shade, or swallowing a cup of coffee. Paralinguistic cues include snorting through the nose, clearing the throat, or gasping. A third type of boundary marker is *silence* with its multifaceted uses.[9]

## Pastoral Listening Guidelines for Groups

Undoubtedly, readers have experienced most of the dynamics just mentioned or have consciously employed some of the techniques as part of their listening behaviors. What, then, does this mean for the pastoral leader-listener? Several things demand that the leader-listener be a student of listening in groups. First, listening involves learning and interpreting the nonverbal environment created by the participation of others in the meeting. Second, it means being conversant with basic group dynamics in order to know what to avoid and what to capitalize on in creating active, positive listening contexts.

Finally, listening in groups means that vocationally the priest is "under call" to use these human communication dynamics in specific biblical, theological, and pastoral ways. This is sometimes a profoundly strenuous task when the democratic, freewheeling nature of the church manifests itself with the "everyone has a voice" approach, and biblically "the very least of these" has a voice!

Vocationally, the minister is called on to listen in meetings, keeping in mind the following:

*1. All forms of active, honest listening should be directed at building up the body of Christ.*

This includes meetings that contain significant conflict, lack of resolution, positive results, or ambiguous outcomes. One seminary president was recently asked how he could endure the hours of listening he was called on to do in long meetings, which, in fact, seemed to relish ineffective floundering and struggle on the part of participants. His response was, "I love to see people finally arrive at good resolutions of issues, however long it takes, for the sake of the church."

The listening modeled by the pastoral leader must extend to all meetings in the parish and for as long as he or she is present in that assembly. Active listening transcends any one meeting context, encouraging parishioners to believe that they can try again and with better results next time.

### 2. Pastoral leadership listening requires the listener to always ask herself or himself and sometimes the group, "What is going on here among us theologically?"

This is a double stipulation for the pastoral listener: good listening is required, but it must also be with a critical frame of theological interpretation. It is one thing to think about theology in the course of doing ministry and quite another to frame human transactions through thoughtful theologizing. Good listening offers an invaluable course in learning what perspectives constitute the body of Christ in a given locale for pastor and people.

### 3. Active, honest pastoral leadership means listening to all elements represented in the parish.

Real or perceived partisan listening in the pastoral office is deadly to the life of a parish. Ministers are theologically and vocationally under obligation to listen to the entire body of Christ, however that expresses itself. Obviously, it matters how one responds, but the initial vocational imperative is always: Listen to the people of God! This means that the pastor will continually negotiate the awesome historical demands and traditions of listening-as-obedience (so easy to impose by pastoral leadership!) with listening that does not and should not connote obedience to the speaker's needs. A minister who takes pastoral listening to heart will probably never listen to the parish and find he or she is hearing those without a voice because of an earlier pastoral refusal to hear them.

### 4. Healthy pastoral listening involves consciousness of networking.

It is both naïve and unwise to think that the listening a minister does in a meeting is restricted only to those physically present. Individuals in parish meetings represent diverse viewpoints; they may be married to or friends with those who hold different perspectives, they may find they are representing unfavorable ideas, or they may feel caught between views or groups. They may represent ideas that belong to other constituencies outside the parish, favorable or not. All of these spoken or unspoken relationships influence pastoral listening and continue outside the meeting itself. While the inevitable networking is represented in the meeting, later it will reconfigure itself in the community based on the kind of listening participants feel they have experienced from their leadership. Listening to the community speak to its various parts is a strengthening strategy on the part of the minister.

*5. If the minister wishes to change and improve her or his listening skills, it is only ethical to share that fact and the process with those in the group.*

It is important that the pastor inform others that changes are afoot, and what listening procedures are being enacted. If they are not warned, people will sense changes in meeting dynamics that can be interpreted as manipulative or confusing. Sudden silences where none existed before is an example of a change that might cause problems. The major advantage of sharing information about listening skills is that participants can join in the learning process as well. There are some programs in parish life that do, in fact, teach listening skills to parishioners, such as the Stephen Ministries.[10] Certainly informed listeners will make better meeting participants! However, there is a deeper reason for encouraging all parishioners to learn basic listening skills: it is at the heart of a deepened spiritual life.

*6. Pastoral discernment of roadblocks: what are parishioners unable or unwilling to hear?*

A minister's stay in a parish will, over time, present a profile not only of what parishioners hear but also of those repeated neuralgic, threatening, or painful issues that they cannot listen to. In specifically identifying these places of painful deafness, the minister may begin the pastoral work of listening equipped with ways to enable participants to hear, perhaps for the first time, some of the deepest issues of the faith community. A significant and familiar example comes from those dying parishes once possessed of large Sunday schools—the "hope of the future." Parish planning, discussion, and publicity may all continue to promote a vision of parish education that counters the reality of an aging parish. But how can the pastor assist a dying parish to face the realities of its own aging process so that people listen and flourish? That, of course, is only one part of the question. Mixing metaphors, one must also ask: How does the minister monitor his or her own listening blind spots?

## A Pastoral Listening Exercise

The following grid, applied to ministry listening and based on the Wolvin-Coakley taxonomy, can serve several purposes. First, in using the pastoral grid, one can list items for an individual in much the same way as the Wolvin-Coakley grid and specify those areas that are strong or weak or to which the listener brings particular interest or talents. Second, the minister can use the grid to construct a corporate chart of parish listening patterns—not as they could be, but as they are. This would involve pinpointing problem areas, areas of strength, and, if possible, the ways these areas impact the parish's programs and relationships. Finally, the results of the parish and pastoral charts may be used as part of any parish education on listening, such as in the area of preaching.

### A Pastoral Listening Grid

| | God | Self | Conversation | Small Group | Worship | Confessional/ Therapeutic | Community |
|---|---|---|---|---|---|---|---|
| Discriminative | | | | | | | |
| Comprehensive | | | | | | | |
| Therapeutic | | | | | | | |
| Critical | | | | | | | |
| Appreciative | | | | | | | |

# A Test Case:
# A Pastor Listens to a Staff Member

During the pastors' listening course at Gettysburg Lutheran Seminary, the participants worked on listening projects in their ministry settings.[11] The following pages contain excerpts from one pastor's efforts to listen better at staff meetings by using the Wolvin-Coakley listening typology.[12] The pastor's staff included a full-time director of children and youth ministries, a part-time church musician, a part-time parish administrator, and a full-time parish secretary. The pastor taped two of the meetings (with the participants' knowledge) and used the information for the project. The following excerpts show some of the insights the pastor gained in the way the meetings were conducted in terms of listening.

## First Meeting

*As I listened to the tape of the meeting and to my responses, I realized that the basic method of listening in which I engage during these meetings was comprehensive. . . . I also thought about the basic tone of the staff meetings and my own attitude during the meetings. I wanted to keep the meetings as short as possible, exchange only information necessary for the ongoing work of the staff.*

*Information concerning discriminative listening was also helpful . . . since the purpose of the meeting is strictly businesslike, it raised questions for me of why we held it in the parlor rather than in the meeting room. What, if anything, was I trying to convey with this choice of surroundings? Was I trying to counter the tone by holding the meeting in more comfortable surroundings?*

*Part of my anxiety stemmed from my attempt to control the talking of the one staff member without having her feeling she had been cut off, and to keep the meeting moving so that the other staff person would not feel her time had been wasted. In the midst of all of this, somehow did I lose sight of why we needed this time together?*

*Another interesting point is that even though information may have been exchanged . . . miscommunication still occurred more than it should. Since memory plays an important part in comprehensive listening, I know this needs to be studied.*

*The most important question is, if I want staff meetings to be different, how must I change my listening in order to effect a change in the staff meetings?*

To begin, I planned to share some of this information with the staff at the beginning of the next meeting and to ask for their response. Do they feel my perceptions concerning the tone and pace of the meetings are correct? What is it they need from staff meetings? Should more information and envisioning be shared within this meeting rather than in individual meetings?

For my part, I will attempt to ask more open-ended questions and to bring into staff meetings some of the skills of therapeutic listening: attentiveness, supportive climate, a willingness to listen, and a desire to understand. Although I use these skills constantly in interactions with parishioners, I tend to be different with the staff.

## Second Meeting

I asked them, as the staff meetings have been structured, what have been their purposes? [Following a time of sharing] I explained that as I reflected on the staff meetings and how I listen, I sensed a feeling of time limitation, that the goal seemed to be to get in there, share the information quickly, and get out as soon as possible. Again, I reiterated that this may be my own anxiety and not theirs.

I explained that there are different levels of listening and that one of these levels was simply the exchange of information such as takes place during briefings. But if there is something else we could be doing with our staff meetings or need to do, then we may want to shift a bit.

I then asked them about when we share information: "Do all of you feel as though you're tuned in to what other staff are doing to the extent that you need to be? We don't need to know everything . . . but do you feel that enough information is shared?" The staff affirmed that they felt they were informed.

I was especially observant during this meeting, noting not only my own responses but also the interaction of the staff. I intentionally continued to bring into the meeting therapeutic skills as I had intended. Although the staff had indicated that they perceived no anxiety or problems with the meeting, this meeting was decidedly different. Without exception, all the staff shared more information in a relaxed way. Staff was more involved in mutual problem solving and in affirming one another. There was also more humor.

What I have learned from intentionally observing the meetings and in paying more attention to my listening skills is that how I listen greatly affects staff meetings. While the staff may not have been aware of certain dynamics in the meetings, by changing my listening behavior, I observed a noticeable change in the staff meeting. I would assume that these learnings would carry over to other meetings within the church.

# A Quaker Form of Corporate Listening

An unusual way of listening in groups comes from the Quaker tradition. Parker J. Palmer describes it as a "clearness committee." The type of listening that Palmer advocates is a hybrid of critical-therapeutic levels of listening and involves three or more people. It is a form of group discernment; the format could easily be used for settings other than therapeutic ones. As part of a parish listening program, it provides a unique way to learn the discipline of listening and may be used periodically with those pastoral and laity support structures that are sometimes mandated by the church's parish or national constitution. This is how it works.

People who may be lay or ordained share the listening task. Palmer says, "We would grow as individuals and communities if we had responsible structures for dealing with our dilemmas in the company of a few friends . . . without feeling intimidated by their lack of 'professional expertise.'"[13] The theological rationale behind such a committee is this: "Each of us has an inner, divine light that gives us the guidance we need but is often obscured by sundry forms of inner and outer interference. The function of the clearness committee is not to give advice or alter and 'fix' people but to help people remove obstacles and discover the divine assistance that is within."[14] The tools the committee uses to arrive at this are "silence, through questioning, though listening, through prayer."[15] The following are the working steps Palmer lays out for the committee: First, "the person seeking clearness begins by writing down his or her situation in advance of the meeting and circulating the statement to members of the committee."[16] Then "the focus person chooses his or her committee—five or six trusted individuals with as much diversity among them as possible."[17] A chair and a recording secretary are appointed. After that, the "meeting begins with a period of centering silence. When the focus person is ready, he or she begins with a fresh summary of the question or issue. Then the committee speaks, governed by a simple but difficult and demanding rule: Members must limit themselves to asking the focus person questions. . . . This means no advice. . . . Nothing is allowed except authentic, challenging, open, loving *questions*."[18] "Committee members should try to ask questions briefly and to the point."[19] "The focus person normally responds to the questions as they are asked . . . and the responses generate more questions."[20] "It is *always* the focus person's absolute right *not* to answer."[21] "The pace of the questioning and answering . . . should be relaxed, gentle, humane."[22] "The clearness committee works best when everyone approaches it in a prayerful . . . mood. . . . We must give up the arrogance that we are obliged to 'save' each other and simply try, through prayerful attentiveness, to establish the conditions in which we can be open to God's saving work."[23]

## Summary

Groups that meet regularly have well-established listening patterns, whether they know it or not. A first step in good group meetings is to acquaint oneself with what these dynamics appear to be. This may seem an obvious first step in a new ministry setting, but ministers will be surprised at what is yet to be learned in parishes they have served for a longer time. In either case, it may take a while to establish what other hidden listening structures are also at work; for example, how people are listening in worship. Such insights can be gained both through the pastor's observations and by asking parishioners how they characterize their listening patterns: the frames used, expected patterns of civility, and what they also cannot or do not wish to hear. As a result, the minister can develop a picture of the contours of his or her own and the parish's listening habits and how these are enacted in parish programs and relationships.

As the minister works with various parish groups, a long-term part of his or her vocational duties as a minister is to heighten awareness, to identify, and to provide instruction in listening techniques that can contribute to a deepened communal parish life. In initiating the personal and corporate education process for better listening, the leader-listener may wish to begin with a single group, such as a staff or a therapeutic listening group similar to the one described by Parker Palmer.

## For Discussion

1. How would you describe or chart the listening habits of your given faith community?

2. What frameworks does the community use, acknowledged or otherwise, to listen?

3. What patterns of civility apply regarding who speaks? When? How often? What are the signaling mechanisms individuals use to listen or to speak? What does this say about the power structures of the community?

4. What presents the greatest challenge to listening/hearing in your group meetings?

5. Would you add any other vocational imperatives for better listening in groups?

6. How does chairing the major meetings in your ministry setting affect the listener's role?

7. How do you/the group handle those who are not adept at turn-taking in meetings?

8. Who are the good or even the best listeners in your parish setting? In what ways have they established their reputations as good listeners?

9. What is at stake theologically in changing current listening habits for yourself and your parish?

10. Are there any types of parish programs in your church that contain elements of listening education?

11. In which meetings would you start the minister/parishioner listening education process? Why?

12. What powers does an acute listener have in a group? Is an acute listener the same as a good listener?

*Eight*

# Listening in Community: Fragility and Watchfulness

To "listen" another's soul into a condition of disclosure and discovery may be almost the greatest service that any human being ever performs for another.

          —Douglas V. Steere, *On Listening to Another*

The type of listening described in this chapter deals with what most ministers understand as "therapeutic listening." Wolvin and Coakley define this as "listening to provide a troubled sender with the opportunity to talk through a problem."[1] It builds on the basic skills of discriminative and comprehensive listening. Therapeutic listening especially emphasizes these elements of our definition of pastoral listening: "emerging from vocational and faith identity . . . subject to pertinent societal and ecclesiastical boundaries . . . both individual and corporate in nature."

As our survey of pastoral theological/counseling books demonstrates, while many people believe that pastors are educated in listening skills, this belief is not supported by the written evidence. For example, a current encyclopedia on pastoral counseling contains two entries related to listening. The first shows little awareness of listening skills beyond the mention of a 1936 work distinguishing active and passive listening. The section on evaluation and diagnosis from a religious perspective does not mention listening at all![2]

Those who lead denominational judicatories—bishops, presidents, and so on—can attest to the numerous failures of communications caused by poor pastoral listening skills, especially therapeutic listening skills. One rightfully frustrated bishop remarked, "Pastor X's congregation is suffering because of his repeated violations of confidences. And yet he doesn't think he has a problem. Why do pastors do this? I can only conclude it's a matter of inappropriate power use and ego."

In this chapter, therapeutic listening will be discussed from several perspectives. The goal is not to offer instructions for pastoral counseling, which can be found in various pastoral resources. Instead, the following materials are provided as a means of assisting the pastoral leader to construct a corporate style of listening, inclusive of individual listening contexts, that takes into account a variety of factors.

First, for purposes of comparison, three contemporary descriptions of pastoral therapeutic listening skills are cited. The sources are Wolvin and Coakley, Wood, and Egan. They provide a cluster of perspectives on therapeutic listening that will enable ministers to compare and contrast their own understandings of therapeutic listening. Next, a look at some typical listening contexts will be shared through two projects from the listening course that demonstrated pastoral uses of and reflections on therapeutic listening. Third, the Wolvin-Coakley definition will be expanded in order to explore the types of pastoral listening that are therapeutically oriented toward issues of a corporate/congregational nature. This includes a look at the therapeutic listening role that gossip plays in a parish and the connection between therapeutic listening and social justice advocacy.

## Three Definitions of Therapeutic Listening Skills

Each of the major listening frameworks below has been researched in depth, at least from a skills perspective.[3] They offer the reader an opportunity to view the many facets of therapeutic listening skills as well as noting those that may be most compatible with the minister's own setting. Note that the perspectives vary according to a number of factors: the extent to which suggested listening skills and patterns begin with a focus on the counselor or the counselee; the theological work involved in the nonverbal, paraverbal, and verbal factors; and the vocabulary used to describe listening.

First, Wolvin and Coakley name these necessary skills in therapeutic listening: "focusing attention, demonstrating attending behaviors, developing a supportive communication climate, listening with empathy, and responding appropriately."[4]

Wood describes pastoral listening in this way:

- There is the empathic hearing of what is being communicated, through the verbal means available to the discloser, and nonverbal and contextual messages. Empathic listening moves into the world of feeling and meaning of the discloser with the goal of accurate understanding.

- There is listening from a theological perspective, that is paying attention to where and how the disclosures pertain to theological themes: faith, providence, grace, repentance, communion, vocation, creatureliness, the holy.

- One must listen to the self as listener, paying attention to the affects and effects of the disclosures. These three facets are in continuous interplay.[5]

Egan describes listening under the header "Active Listening" and lists these four main areas: listening to and understanding nonverbal behavior; verbal messages; clients in context; and tough-minded listening, defined as "detecting the gaps, distortions, and dissonance that are part of the client's experienced reality."[6] He also describes listening in two other sections: "The Shadow Side of Listening to Clients" and "Listening to Oneself."[7]

Therapeutic pastoral listening skills are brought to bear on typical parish situations of counseling and crisis counseling. The type of person seeking a therapeutic listener will usually represent the constituency of the faith community served, with the listening contextualized accordingly.

Who comes for therapeutic listening? The answers are as numerous as potential human situations. Some listening settings may occur once with a person or persons, and others may continue for months. Some situations are mildly problematic while others are in *extremis*. Ministers may be comfortable with one type of setting and find others distasteful. The pastoral listener may believe that she is doing a good job in one setting, while not being heard or hearing inadequately in others. Churches may structure the listening formally, as in liturgical confession, or it may occur in a more informal conversational setting. In any event, therapeutic listening is probably the one type of listening ministers are expected to do the most.

# Two Therapeutic Listening Settings

Therapeutic listening is strenuous. Excerpts from two course projects describe this kind of listening in two typical pastoral settings: one is visiting a shut-in and the other relates to chaplaincy work in a hospice setting. Both writers draw on the Wolvin-Coakley listening taxonomy to explain their listening processes. Both are ordained pastors, and their projects reflect their efforts at integrating listening skills into their work as theologians.[8]

## Listening to a Shut-in

**The Listening Situation.** *Although visitation ministry has been a consistently strong and enjoyable part of ministry for me, I have fallen into a pattern of calling upon shut-in and institutionalized people (hospitalized or nursing home resident) late in the day when the ability to concentrate on other tasks has begun to wane.*

*I recognize a "down time" in the daily rhythm of my mental energy that generally occurs in the mid-afternoon. And since this is also a down time at many care facilities, with tests and therapy sessions generally finished for the day, it has always seemed a convenient time to make such visits. Because this time coincides with the nadir of my own daily energy cycle, it occurred to me that perhaps also my listening skills were not at their sharpest for these visits. If that is true, then I must either reinvigorate myself and give greater attention to listening skills at these times, or rearrange my schedule so that the sick and home bound receive the attention they need and deserve from me.*

**The Baseline Goal.** *For the initial visit, my goals were to practice comprehensive listening and therapeutic listening. Special attention was given to concentration on the conversation and the blocking out of distractions. Primary here is the TV. Betty lives alone, and the TV is on almost constantly in the kitchen (and we generally visit at the kitchen table). Even when Betty is not in the room and attentive to the program, the TV remains on to provide some noise and a type of companionship. Because the TV is a constant presence, she is much better able to block it out. Part of the agenda for this initial visit was to bring the Lord's Supper and share a word of Scripture. This first visit took place later in the Lenten season.*

*Several contacts, all of a passing nature, were made in the two weeks that intervened between the first and second visit. The second visit was made on the Second Sunday of Easter. The goal of the second visit was to utilize more critical listening skills in combination with therapeutic listening skills. It was apparent from the first visit that Betty spends considerable energy rationalizing her current situation. Her life has changed dramatically, and she is seeking to justify her changed circumstances.*

Discoveries. *It was much easier to remember the conversation that concerned Betty herself, her own health, recent visits to the doctor. It was much more difficult to remember the parts of the conversations that concerned other people (both those known to us and those who are friends of Betty). Giving more attention to concentration in a sense disproved my initial premise—that listening suffered in my down time of day. The late afternoon visit and the early Sunday afternoon visit were very much the same in terms of what was remembered afterwards.*

*It proved rather difficult to hold off critical listening skills for the second visit, practicing more the discriminative skills during the first visit. Some of the things Betty said needed to be challenged; for example, her reasons for her continued isolation. I was not entirely successful in holding off such challenges in our first encounter. In part this was because our conversation went in directions that such responses were possible. I was not entirely sure that such opportunities would present themselves again. At the risk of becoming judgmental, Betty has become very dependent and also rather demanding. It seems to me that she is using her medical situation to manipulate others and to hold at a distance those who would encourage her to "get with it."*

## Listening in a Hospice Setting

[The writer, as a hospice chaplain, fills out a "Spiritual Assessment Form" (SAF) as part of his work. Securing the information for the form draws on his listening skills in a variety of ways.]

*This piece (SAF) is filled out during or after one of my first visits with each client. It makes the attempt to summarize the spiritual orientation of the client and significant other. It also lists information about any religious institution or congregation with which they are affiliated, and* allows for information supplied by the spiritual caregiver(s) from that body. While the form cannot replace dialogue among team members, it makes a quick reference sheet. It also provides a starting point for me as I get to know each new unit of care.

Discriminative listening can be a real challenge with hospice/home health clients. Most will happily turn off the television. Fans and air conditions are a must for many of our folks. Oxygen and suction machines abound. Pets break the ice, but some are noisy. The same is true about youngsters. The phone or doorbell may ring. Even body sounds may interfere with hearing. I need to gauge how and whether I should ask that a distracting sound be removed.

Comprehensive listening is entwined with the discriminative in the assessment process. Some individuals suffer from speech impairment. Not only are they difficult to understand, but often their significant others feel they must answer for these clients. Still others suffer from cognitive disability, even advanced dementia. I must work to pay close attention to verbal and nonverbal communication. Watching individuals' lips and other facial features helps me understand unclear words. Often I lean in close. Pointing and gesturing become appropriate on both sides of the conversation. Much of the time it is well to wait quietly until a distraction passes or a patient is able, slowly and with pauses, to express him, or herself. My pace must slow and my mental reactivity must be reined in, even when other thought processes are alert. I may have to search for the emotion or nuance behind a person's short statement, because pitch and volume are determined by physical illness.

Therapeutic listening operates in a primary and secondary mode during the spiritual assessment visit. One quality of therapeutic listening is that it draws out the other. Certainly I hope to do that, so that I can more adequately gather information, and also so that the client has some opportunity to grow in understanding of him- or herself during this conversation.

I will want to employ therapeutic listening to find out specifically what the client fears (pain, suffocation, etc.), but then what will probably help them most is to give them information about the dying process and how hospice will make them as comfortable as possible through it. I may also tell them that all the hospice deaths I have attended have been comfortable. The challenge is not to cut off the client by giving information prematurely.

*Appreciative listening has more to do with how I believe God looks at each individual than how I, in my humanness, want to critically analyze what I've learned about him or her. Eventually I will need to think about whether this person's theology is going to hold up during the dying process. Even now I may note "red flags" that warn me that a particular individual may face real distress about God's role in life and death. I am simply trying to find out what that personal theology is, and furthermore, to appreciate how it has functioned for the individual.*

In both case studies, the clergy involved made a conscious effort to identify various types of listening. Their reflections demonstrate that their ability to understand their listening processes greatly enriched their own sense of ministry in a given situation, as well as giving them a greater self-awareness about their own listening capacities.

## Listening Corporately

### The Role of Gossip

The Wolvin-Coakley definition of therapeutic listening focuses on two elements: the individual speaker and the speaker's problem ("trouble"). There are, however, other types of therapeutic listening that the minister might do of a corporate nature. This has been identified in our principal definition of pastoral listening, specifically related to: "subject to pertinent societal and ecclesiastical boundaries . . . and corporate in nature."

As mentioned earlier, any individual conversation in a faith community with a pastoral listener presupposes the backdrop of the entire community; in theological terms, the body of Christ or the communion of saints. As such, ministerial listening at this level is consistently multi-contextual. The pastoral listener is always listening to the group he or she serves, however conscious of that he or she may be. Listening to another individual's conversation must be considered separately as well as a part of the larger context.

One important way that the connections between an individual speaker and others can be known is through the exchange of information—ongoing in any ministry setting—generally called "gossip." It may seem strange or even contradictory to understand gossip as a form of therapeutic listening/speaking! That is, however, one of its many functions. It is usually defined in a negative fashion, but, in fact, it can also signify support and information exchange in a congregation; both dimensions will be examined here. The pastoral listener must be cognizant of this ongoing part of parish life and attend to its ramifications, lest he or she be the only stranger in Jerusalem that is unaware of key events. Without an appreciation of the role of gossip, the clergy leader has lost access to an important form of internal parish communication.

The dictionary describes the etymology and first three definitions of gossip this way: Gossip (noun) comes from the Old English *godsibb*, which means godparent; 1. a person spiritually related to another through being his sponsor at baptism; 2. a friend or companion; 3. a person who habitually retails facts, rumors or behind-the-scenes information of an intimate, personal, or sensational nature.

Gossip has been studied as a form of human communication with some surprising insights. Luckmann defines it as "a genre of moral communication in a twofold sense: it moralizes and is moralized about." Gossip in a community then does several things, according to Luckmann: "The analysis of gossip reveals much about the oral order of a society and even more about the communicative construction and maintenance of that order. . . . it [can] be considered a laboratory case for the study of the construction of social relationships, of the drawing of boundaries between a We and a They, of the creation of moral solidarities, and of shifting alignments."[9]

The following excerpts should aid the pastoral listener in dealing with gossip at a corporate level. Features of the one gossiped about, the one who gossips, and the one who receives the information form a gossip triad; they are summarized below.

First, who is gossiped about? Bergmann says that the subject of gossip is characterized by excluding from conversation the one talked about who is only "present" as discussed. Further, the reason gossip occurs is because people keep secrets. In other words, what we see publicly of an individual is not the subject of gossip. It is the tension between what is seen and the "secrets" of the private life that yields gossip.[10] Bergmann sums this up by saying, "Absence, acquaintanceship, and privacy . . . are the three constitutive features of the figure of the subject of gossip."[11]

Second, what characterizes the gossiper, the one talking? Bergmann describes his actions of gossip in this way:

[T]he gossip producer is a "transgressor" in two senses: he penetrates—by crossing the border between the back stage and proscenium—the inner space of another's social existence and then—disdaining the social system of inclusion and exclusion for the time being—pushes outward with his information as the booty of his raid. Expressed paradoxically, the gossip producer externalizes what is internal. His reputation and position within the gossip triad is essentially determined by the potential and factual access he has to the unequally distributed information about another's private life and the extent to which the dissemination of this information is subject to socially enforced restrictions.[12]

Finally, what of the one receiving the information, the gossip recipient? Bergmann says, "Information about another's private affairs is morally contaminated information and thereby places those who exchange it in a relationship of co-informers."[13] In other words, the gossip is one "who accepts a gift that he as well as the giver knows is stolen."[14] The gossip recipient is also someone who is known to the speaker and therefore reflects "a specific model of intimacy within the relational network of its three participants."[15]

Bergmann's theory of gossiping is summed up in four of his conclusions that identify gossip as a means of social control, a mechanism of preserving social groups, a technique of information management, and the social form of discreet indiscretion.[16] While Bergmann's study shows that gossiping has an obvious unethical side to it, it is nevertheless a form of communication to which the pastor must listen carefully.

In a positive, historical sense, gossip's original definition signifies a spiritual connection among those who speak. As the pastoral leader listens to the individual and to the group, it is important to appreciate the functions gossip plays in a faith community. One listening theorist supports this approach by noting: "Listening for facts only is another bad habit. . . . Facts are important, of course, but more important is what they mean or what they add up to."[17]

## Listening toward Justice

In keeping with this chapter's definition of pastoral therapeutic listening, it is important to ask which groups and individuals are in special need of listening and how therapeutic listening relates to justice. The latter is a crucial consideration, since therapeutic listening is often assumed to be the most "private" of listening venues.

Some often overlooked groups are children, the aged, those with disabilities and illness (observable or hidden), and groups such as gays and lesbians.[18] In some cases jeopardized groups are represented institutionally, through such organizations as Amnesty International and Habitat for Humanity. Listening to such groups has implications far beyond any faith community. As mentioned earlier, one major listening expectation for clergy is the major cultural and theological understanding that they are "called to listen on behalf of other communities; communities and persons with little or no voice; globally, as alert watchers to changes in the public and private sector."[19] Examples of these communities are numerous. Faith groups will often choose to focus on those having some ties to their beliefs or to current events.

As with other groups that may be represented more immediately in the community or congregation, one activity that becomes associated with therapeutic listening is advocacy. The range of issues needing the attention of listening faith communities is enormous. Pastoral listening must not only address these but find ways to encourage their congregations to listen as well. This is not easy; in some cases, it is almost impossible. The pastoral listener who attempts to engage parishioners in advocacy must also be prepared for those who believe they have a choice about what their pastoral leader does or does not listen to. One example is the cluster of issues related to the Holocaust, current hate crimes, and anti-Semitism. In a recent presentation, author Elie Wiesel spoke on the Holocaust and modern memory.[20] He made explicit links between listening and community. The program announcing his presentation contains this passage:

> After the war people did not want to listen to us. Survivors did not speak, not because we did not want to tell the tale. We did not speak because no one wanted to listen, because some would not understand. Others would not believe. So we stopped talking. Why bother people? When I wrote *Night,* I meant it for the survivors first, to say that we must talk even if people do not listen. We must talk. We must tell the tale.[21]

To listen is to identify those who can be brought to speech, those who have stories urgently needing hearing, and to begin doing justice with and for those in need of it. The most crucial issue this raises is how to extend such listening skills, concerns, and directions into the faith community in such a way that pastor and people know theologically what is at stake. This extension of listening skills will be considered in the next chapter as a theology of listening is charted out.

## Summary

Therapeutic listening offers a wealth of definitions. Such listening is assumed by the general populace to be "the minister's job," despite the lack of educational opportunities in this area of communications. The three pastoral perspectives on listening list several contemporary definitions of therapeutic listening. It is essential that the minister also extend definitions of therapeutic listening to the corporate framework, of which individual conversations form only a part. The pastoral case studies mentioned in this chapter demonstrate a keen awareness of how both individuals and others impact the listening setting over a period of time and beyond the core context. This means acknowledging the role corporate listening plays through the major mechanism of gossip and issues of social advocacy, that is, the links between listening and doing justice. This suggests that the private act of listening does have bearing on the well-being of the corporate body of Christ. Moreover, listening to the disenfranchised does not allow the listener the luxury of unresponsiveness.

Since therapeutic listening forms much of a minister's sense of vocation and often determines his or her use of time, it is important to ask if the minister is aware of such listening skills, of the corporate framework in which they are exercised, and of what is at stake theologically.

## For Discussion

1. Have you considered your role as a corporate listener in your ministry setting? If so, how?

2. How do you understand therapeutic listening theologically? Who/what are your role models for this?

3. Do you find yourself in an unusual listening place as a minister? Is there anyone trained in listening skills with whom you can talk?

4. In what areas of the Wolvin-Coakley listening skills do you think you are strongest? Needing improvement? Threatened by?

5. What would you add to your own definition of therapeutic listening?

6. What role does gossip play in your church community in positive and in negative ways? Are there any liturgical, professional, ecclesial ways gossip is dealt with in your faith community in its negative presentations?

7. To what extent does gossip play a therapeutic role in your community?

8. How do you listen to constituencies that are considered fragile in your community and elsewhere?

9. How do you understand the connection between therapeutic listening and doing justice in your ministry setting?

*Nine*

# A Theology of Listening: Attending to the Future

> The search for a listening silence continues nevertheless to attract us in the most unusual ways: The sounding and, we might say, the eloquent silence of truth insinuates itself noiselessly into our minds, writes Augustine.
>
> —Gemma Corradi Fiumara, *The Other Side of Language*

Is it possible to have a theology of listening? Why attempt it? How should it be composed? This chapter is both a summary of and an experiment in first sketches of a theology of listening, weaving together several strands of reflection from the fields of philosophy, speech communications, and theology. The initial definition of pastoral listening developed in this work will help us identify how a theology of listening for ministers can and must construct a healthy listening habitat to be effective. The journey toward further listening studies in theological contexts will conclude the chapter.

## Constructing a Theology of Listening

What is a theology of listening? In these pages, the elements of a listening skills–based approach to pastoral ministry have been proposed and the spectrum of pastoral listening venues described. Such skills, however, are more than the sum of their parts, so it is important to reiterate the theological rationale that motivates the use of these skills and to ask what elements contribute to a theology of listening. This book advocates listening that offers a particular perspective on God and on humanity. At the very center of this theology of listening is a paraphrasing of 1 John 4:19: "We love because God first loved us." A theology of listening understands that "We listen because God first listened to us." Before the Word is the silence, and in that silence is the presence of one who listens.

This theology of listening is active and incarnational; it weds theory and practice and involves community, leadership, ministry, listening, power, silence, and speech. Sadly, such interrelationships have often been ignored or denied. The logos of the Christian tradition is now drowning in the general logocentricity of the culture itself. "Word of God," perfect in its divine balance of speech and silence, is becoming almost indistinguishable from the morass of the words around us.

Adding to the tragedy, as this volume has demonstrated, is the reality that the importance of listening and concomitant listening instruction is lacking in most pastoral training. Examination of theological educational materials of all types supports this belief. And yet, both the tradition of the Christian faith and its daily ministry strongly bear out the fact that—culturally and spiritually—ministers are expected to be listeners as a prior qualification for anything else they might do. If listening training has appeared at all, it has been generally in the fields of pastoral theology and counseling. This leaves open the question of where it has disappeared to in biblical studies, historical studies, doctrinal studies, and administrative training.

Furthermore, the mighty and long-standing constraints of a theological heritage that is primarily known and enacted as logocentric gives only brief accounts of listening. At its worst, listening is assumed, ignored, or focused more on speaking responses as part of the communicative strategies of our tradition. Because it is less easy to identify the stuff of listening, a focus on this practice is sometimes perceived as a passive response or a threshold receptivity to the act of speaking and language.

Resistance to listening is also at heart a spiritual issue: truthful listening is more demanding, calls forth the listener's vulnerabilities, and may result in changes the listener will resist when confronted with new possibilities.

The implications for restricting listening to those areas of pastoral work that usually encounter the suffering, the distressed, or those in crisis raises an interesting question about power. If the minister listens from a clearly advantaged perspective, what are the ramifications of listening

in noncrisis situations with those who clearly have other grounds, perhaps powerful in their own right, on which to build the speaking / listening
relationship?

Certainly, the biblical mandate to listen to the disenfranchised is central to ministry, but what of listening to those who share power, or wish
to do so, in ecclesial settings? This appears to be the more difficult task
for pastoral listeners who may fall short in this area. They often resort to
responses that do not include listening, such as invoking the powers of
the pastoral office; expecting the pastoral word to be received in the traditional sense of "obedience" to the speaker; or simply refusing to listen
at those levels of ministry that are most threatening.

The traditional eclipse and loss of a listening stance in theology and
the contemporary assaults of a logocentric culture are compelling reasons to identify the spaces, gaps, and supposed emptiness to which a
theology of listening invites us.

## Listening in the Philosophical Tradition

Undoubtedly, the construction of a theology of listening owes a debt to
the philosophical thinkers of past and present. They offer resources for
such a theology in their address of issues such as the nature of language,
silence, and the ways we think and perceive reality. However fragmentary,
the philosophical tradition has acknowledged the function of listening
as a matter to be reckoned with from an epistemological perspective.
Many of its contributions can positively influence any Christian theology
that takes listening seriously. Writers such as Heidegger, Wittgenstein,
and Ricouer have also contributed some thinking on listening as they
have dealt with language and its silences.[1]

The primary work in the field of listening today is Gemma Corradi
Fiumara's *The Other Side of Language: A Philosophy of Listening.* She
develops the following points in her argument for a focus on listening
by first exploring the meanings of the word "logos," and concludes we
have missed an important meaning by overlooking its sense of "laydown and laying-before which gathers itself and others."[2]

This points us to "the space," the reality of listening, as the first step
toward reclaiming what Fiumara describes as "a divided logos and its
restoration."[3] She means that through investing in listening, we will be
able to begin the initial step of "creating sufficient silence to allow our

selves at least to hear the incessant rumbling of our cultural world—a machinery of thought that seems to have lost its original vitality as a result of its enormous success."[4]

Fiumara offers a persuasive philosophical case for listening as something that is far beyond merely a threshold for words or an attitude of compassionate passivity. What is particularly important about her analysis is the focus on the corporate problems and implications of non-listening, whether by choice or by what she names as the violence of "benumbment" in the face of contemporary logocentric cultural settings.[5]

Benumbment is the attitude that humans adopt when "we fail, or refuse, to engage in dialogue [that] can lead to response, gratitude, dialogue."[6] It is "the desire for, or fear of, annihilation." In theological terms, our overuse of words may indeed, by our own choice, purposely draw us away or protect us from true community and an encounter with God.

Fiumara's discussion of corporate and cultural epistemological numbing offers ample material for the reflective theologian to understand the role of listening as it relates to other anthropological realities of community—sin, interpersonal relationships, sickness, and despair. Her analysis promotes the theological observation that to have no listeners to the self is despair and that to have no silence in which to listen to God is the loss of salvation. In summary, this philosopher's willingness to challenge the logocentric tradition of Western culture yields rich materials for the reflective theologian.

## Creating a "Listening Habitat"

Elements of the Christian tradition have identified listening in terms of biblical, doctrinal, practical, and contemplative sources. For the most part, however, they are eclipsed by the contemporary template of cultural logocentrism, which has indeed influenced faith life negatively. In constructing a theology of listening, it is important to retrieve listening as a dynamic in the God/human relationship and to explore what this means theologically and anthropologically. Given the obvious intrinsic dialogic nature of listening/speaking, such an exploration is necessarily communal in vision, as relationships between God and humanity and between individuals and groups are explored.

Thus, the creation of a methodology for a listener's theology becomes important. In the listening spaces between God and humanity and among human beings, our manner of listening will or will not result in constructing a theology of listening that is creative and salvific. The heart of our theology of listening must create a positive listening space that I term a *listening habitat*, defined here as a compassionate context in which the divine and human presences are held together in the background of any listening/speaking event.

The how of listening is not the issue. Certainly, our argument for a theology of listening is based on listening skills crucial to the functioning of a listening habitat. This has been covered earlier. Here we are instead concerned with defining the contours of the listening posts that name us, shape us, and continually create us as a community of faith, intent on hearing both the individual and the corporate heart in the presence of God.

Although the ways we listen are obviously influenced by multiple verbal and nonverbal factors, we are called to create a habitat for one another by a commitment to listening responses that befit a theological intentionality. Theodore Reik, in borrowing a phrase from Friedrich Nietzsche, describes this methodology as "listening with the third ear."[7] St. Benedict has called it "the ear of the heart." This is the kind of listening that spiritual and theological formation should hope to instill, cultivate, and recognize.

In weaving together the insights of theological and philosophical inquiry, the elements that are inevitable components of a theology of listening and may create an ecclesial listening habitat appear in our definition of pastoral listening:

> *Good pastoral listening is governed by a basic knowledge and command of listening skills and structures. It is a theological activity, emerging from vocational and faith identity, present in all forms of ministry, and subject to pertinent societal and ecclesiastical boundaries. It can occur at sensory and nonsensory levels and is both individual and corporate in nature.*

What elements are implied or stated in the definition that constitute a theology of listening and that can help create a listening habitat?

I. **Vocation.** Personal and professional vocational commitments to balancing listening and speaking well can create the listening habitat.

The expectations of the speakers toward the pastoral listener are often specific, religiously and culturally formed. It is here that a pastoral minister educated in good listening skills, in the service of an explicit theology of listening, can match more closely the commonly held assumptions of most parishioners about their pastoral listener/leaders.

**2. Presence.** Presence can mean many things in a theology of listening: the presence of God, of the speaker, of the listener(s), and the presence of issues. It may also mean speaking of those not physically present. Speaking within the safety of the listening habitat confirms the reality that "one of the greatest forms of presence is absence." It could also signify the presence of many other factors both wanted and unneeded.

The issue of maintaining presence is intended in a positive sense. Like other dynamics of the listening event, however, it may also work in negative ways. So, above all else, the pastoral listener must be primarily intent upon incarnational listening, exhibiting the divine readiness and presence to the speaker that keeps in view the godly heart of the listening habitat.

In many situations fraught with the unanswerable, a rightly understood form of pastoral presence brings a particular gift to the speaker. It shares a mutually understood definition of listening and does something else: listening as a divinely linked activity, a listening-with-God-present, fills the need for a response when answers are found wanting.

**3. Silence.** Silence is presumed by all these definitions as the basic receptive factor in listening. It is not merely "nothing"; it is rich with meanings, both positive and negative. For one building a theology of listening, silence can be explored liturgically, sacramentally, psychologically, and biblically. In Barbara Brown Taylor's recent work, *When God Is Silent*, she names some of the outposts of silence that God has established for humanity's salvation:

> The God who keeps silence, even when God's own flesh and blood is begging for a word, is the God beyond anyone's control. An answer will come, but not until the silence is complete. And even then, the answer will be given in silence. With the cross and the empty tomb, God has provided us with two events that defy our efforts to domesticate them. Before them, and before the God who is present in them, our most eloquent words turn to dust.[8]

These are theological underpinnings of listening that must constantly "sound" in the mutually shared silences of speaker and listener.

4. Discernment. This word, rich in possibilities, must be revitalized in a theology of listening. It has been generally associated with only certain portions of the Christian tradition, particularly spiritual direction and charismatic gift enactments. Discernment, however, is the ongoing work of the pastoral listener in creating a faithfully constituted listening habitat. A range of listening methodologies enacts it. At its best, the listener may enable the speaker to engage in a mutual listening experience that makes discernment a joint process. Some of the "listening for" that characterizes discerning listening includes listening for patterns, themes, what is not said, the gaps and silences, sour notes, and grace notes—for things besides "the facts" and, in some cases, for the contradictions—for thresholds, for evidences of change, for God and others simultaneously.

Discernment calls for a vulnerability in the pastoral listener that disavows the prideful power of the "solution person" and allows for new insights on the part of the listener as well as the speaker. Furthermore, the process of discernment can range far beyond the listener/speaker context and has corporate ties as well. Corporate discernment is the natural tidewater in a faith community dedicated to creating a healthy listening habitat.

5. Obedient restraint. The definition of pastoral listening created in this volume indicates a multiple monitoring of the listening event. Listening is not defined, however, as blind or dutiful responses to various constraints. As a pastoral leader, one does not listen in an unbounded fashion but with a divine mandate that in turn can both receive and direct the gifts that good listening can create. This divine mandate is the component of a listening theology that makes listening an activity that respects and honors the speaker and is ethical, moral, and faithful.

# The Future of Pastoral Listening Education

The next step is to ask how creation of a healthy listening habitat, as constructive of a theology of listening, connects with actual listening education in daily ministry. Since the emphasis in this volume is always on both the individual ministerial leader and the corporate nature of ministry, one of the key questions becomes how to extend the traditions of listening into the faith community. Here, acknowledgment of the Christian listening traditions becomes a matter of pedagogy /androgogy.[9]

There are places to start. Parishes may instruct their members in the listening skills promoted by such programs as the Stephen Ministries.[10] Listening skills may be taught in leadership settings, in regular parish programs, and in family-oriented programs.[11] Judicatory leaders can also take a strong hand in establishing listening as a topic for retreats addressing spiritual needs and ministry skills. The topic of listening can provide the subject for Bible studies, preparation of a congregation to listen to liturgy and preaching, and congregational retreats.

Pastoral leaders must ask where they can find good listening education programs and find other options if such programs are not available locally. Four years ago the first seminary course on listening—conducted separately instead of being a part of other theology courses—was offered at Gettysburg Lutheran Theological Seminary. The course syllabus and project description are reprinted in appendix C. It represents a first attempt, to my knowledge, to construct a theological approach to listening based on speech communication theories of listening and speaking.

The co-teachers, one a pastor and homiletician and the other, Norma Schweitzer Wood, a psychologist, instructor, and therapist, combined insights from the individual and corporate components of their own experiences in their teaching. Both of us were consistently struck by the untapped resources of our students and their ministries—they can offer so much to the church in the creation of a theology of listening for ministry.

Whether clergy or laity, the process of learning to listen and the mutual blessings of creating a listening habitat for one another is a claim placed upon us from the Listener who is both the silence and the Word. In conclusion, what is at stake is learning to listen to the love of God. In doing so, pastoral leaders will both learn (and re-learn) to model the fact that true listening is an act of love—divine and human. Learning to listen is preparation for the astonishment of grace and love.

# Summary

Creating a theology of listening is dependent upon the resources of the Christian tradition and the contributions of a handful of philosophers. Its primary aim is to provide a theological rationale for creating good pastoral leader-listeners and enabling them, with their faith communities, to create a healthy listening habitat. This habitat is characterized by several elements that form and contribute to listening and are drawn from a number of different strands of the faith tradition. Undoubtedly, learning to listen better will create change and challenge for all who choose to involve themselves with it.

In order to instruct pastoral leadership in listening skills, venues of theological education—seminaries, synod retreats, continuing education events, training seminars—must incorporate an approach to listening that is consistently theological and ongoing.

# For Discussion

1. What components would you name that are part of your own theology of listening?

2. Why would individuals and congregations resist a theology of listening?

3. How would you describe the listening habitat you offer to others?

4. In what ways has your faith community used or avoided silence?

5. Where would you seek or initiate training in pastoral leadership listening skills?

6. If you wish to explore a theology of listening in your church, with which group would you begin this work? Why?

7. What steps would you outline for a congregation in a listening learning program?

# Appendix A

*Historical View of Pastoral Theology Books on Listening*

|  | Mentioned | Defined | Skills Enumerated |
|---|---|---|---|
| Dietrich Bonhoeffer (1930s) | 0 | 0 | 0 |
| Seward Hiltner (1958) | 0 | 0 | 0 |
| Howard Clinebell (1966, 1984) | X | X | 0 |
| Paul Pruyser (1976) | 0 | 0 | 0 |
| Wayne Oates (1982) | X | X | 0 |
| Thomas Oden (1983) | X | 0 | 0 |
| John Patton (1983) | X | X | 0 |
| Charles Gerkin (1991) | 0 | 0 | 0 |
| Charles Taylor (1991) | X | X | 0 |
| Gerard Egan (1995) | X | X | X |
| James Ashbrook (1996) | 0 | 0 | 0 |
| Christine Cozad Neuger (1996) | X | 0 | 0 |

# Appendix B

*Pastoral Letter*

Dear Friends in Christ:

Last semester I took a course at the Gettysburg Seminary called "Listening." At first I thought, as perhaps you do, that listening is such a basic activity that it would be superfluous to teach a course about it. However, as I came to find out, listening is in fact a complex process and, with some study and practice, we can become better listeners.

Listening is defined as the process of receiving, attending to, and assigning meanings to sounds and visual stimuli. The authors of the text we used in class said repeatedly that the listener is responsible for 51 percent of any communication! Being a better listener is important to us for many reasons. For instance, it is estimated that 60 percent of all commercial airline accidents can be attributed to poor communication in the cockpit. Also, diseases have sometimes been diagnosed incorrectly because the person taking the medical information does not listen well. And the most common complaint spouses have about one another is "He/she doesn't listen to me!" (I would guess that's probably true for parents and children, and employers and employees, too.)

I shared some of what I learned in the listening course with our adult Sunday school classes. One of the things we discussed, which is of great interest to me, was how to improve our sermon listening skills. I have a few suggestions on that topic.

The quality of one's listening experience is often dependent on one's attitude and preparation. First, I would suggest quiet, prayerful, unhurried preparation before the service begins. This might include getting to your pew as early as possible, taking time to pray, of course, and perhaps also looking over your bulletin or reading the lessons, before enjoying the Prelude. This, I believe, can help create an atmosphere of calm receptivity.

You may also want to be sure to take a seat near the front of the church so that you may hear and see (a lot of communication is non-verbal) the preacher better. Get comfortable and remove, or move away from, anything that might distract you, especially disquieting thoughts about other subjects. Don't be afraid to send the preacher feedback through facial expressions, or leaning forward, or laughing when appropriate. Be expectant, be focused: this is God's Word being proclaimed, after all, and you should expect the sermon to have a specific call or challenge or insight for your life. Jot down notes, if you are so inclined, or outline the sermon in your mind, paying particular attention to major points and transitions. Most of all, listen in an opportunistic way. That is, listen for what you need to hear: a word of forgiveness, a word of acceptance, a word of love.

I hope these thoughts are helpful to your sermon listening experience. Thanks for all your good attention.

—Pastor Eric Ash

# Appendix C

*Listening Course Syllabus*

Listening
Spring semester, 1997
Instructors: Dr. Susan K. Hedahl and Dr. Norma S. Wood

I. Rationale
In many ways, listening is foundational to pastoral ministry and has often been underappreciated as an essential dimension of ministry. Not simply an act, effective listening is a relational way of being and a complexity of knowledge, skills, and practice. By exploring the subject of listening from a variety of perspectives and contexts, inclusive of individualized parish listening projects, this course seeks to reclaim its importance in pastoral ministry.

II. Objectives
At the conclusion of the course, the participant will demonstrate capabilities in:
- Articulating the process and role of listening communication.
- Listening more effectively.
- Identifying the biblical basis and role of listening/hearing as constitutive of one's relationship with God and humanity.
- Discerning, practicing the different types of listening available to speakers and hearers.
- Fashioning and evaluating a ministry-based listening project.

III. Strategies
The required text is Andrew Wolvin and Carolyn Gwynn Coakley, *Listening*, 5th ed. (Brown and Benchmark, 1996).

Participants will:
- Cover the assigned materials in Wolvin-Coakley.
- Identify modes of listening situated in various ministry settings.

- Develop and carry out a personal listening project in the parish.
- Prepare a written report and evaluation of it, and present to the class.
- Engage in a variety of in-class listening exercises (ungraded).

Class Schedule

| | |
|---|---|
| Week one | Introduction to the course |
| | Discussion of listening project |
| | The Bible and listening/hearing |
| | In-class practicum |
| Week two | Understanding the listening process, Wolvin/Coakley, pp. 5–143 |
| | In-class practicum |
| Week three | Discriminative listening, Wolvin/Coakley, pp. 157–201 |
| | In-class practicum, pp. 189–99; # 3, 4, 10, 11, 12, 14 |
| Week four | Comprehensive Listening, Wolvin/Coakley, pp. 211–56 |
| | In-class practicum |
| Week five | Therapeutic listening, Wolvin/Coakley, pp. 263–304. |
| Break | No class |
| Week six | Critical listening, Wolvin/Coakley, pp. 309–57 |
| | In-class practicum |
| Week seven | Appreciative listening, Wolvin/Coakley, pp. 363–80 |
| | Contemplative listening |
| | In-class practicum |
| Week eight | Proclamation as listening |
| | The listener's communication roles, Wolvin/Coakley, pp. 385–413 |
| | In-class practicum |
| Week nine | Project presentations |
| Week ten | Project presentations |

IV. Evaluation

STM participants will receive a letter grade based on their overall class participation and on their listening project written report and oral presentation to the class. Instructors will look for demonstration of the course objectives. The listening project is described in more detail as follows:

Course Listening Project

The purpose of the listening project is as follows:
- to focus your attention on listening as a specific dimension of ministry
- to increase your awareness and practice of listening skills in a particular context
- to reflect on the effectiveness and theological significance of listening

Select an area of ministry on which to focus, practice, and evaluate listening behaviors, such as education, administration, visitation, counseling, worship, or outreach. Choose two occasions of engagement in that select area, for example, two meetings of the Stephen ministers' training or two church council meetings.

Use the first meeting to simply observe and describe the types of listening in that meeting and reflect on the effectiveness of that listening. (You will need to devise appropriate methods and tools to assist you in the process of observing and evaluating, for example, using an audio or video tape recording or comparing your verbatim and journaling with feedback from a second observer of the meeting, etc.)

On the basis of your study and evaluation of this first meeting plan, in the second meeting be more deliberate in your focus and practice of listening. Use one or several identified listening modes from Wolvin-Coakley, for example, "I wish to practice discriminative listening in the context of _____ and thereby sharpen my skills in _____."

Following the second meeting, again reflect on your practice of listening and its effectiveness in the meeting. Be sure to pay attention to the pertinent elements of intrapersonal and interpersonal listening, and if the listening project so lends itself, to the elements of public or media communication. Include your evaluation of your engagement in the project, its theological significance, and its value to your ministry.

Prepare a written report and make it available to the instructors and the class. Present your report orally and discuss it with the class as scheduled.

# Notes

## Preface

1. Taylor Caldwell, *The Listener* (New York: Doubleday, 1960).
2. Andrew Wolvin and Carolyn Gwynn Coakley, *Listening*, 5th ed. (Madison: Brown & Benchmark, 1996).

## Introduction

1. "Listening is the first language skill that we develop, and it is followed by other language skills in this order: 1. Listening; 2. Speaking; 3. Reading; 4. Writing." From Andrew Wolvin and Carolyn Gwynn Coakley, *Listening*, 5th ed. (Madison: Brown & Benchmark, 1996), 13, quoting Sara W. Lundsteen, *Listening: Its Impact on Reading and the Other Language Arts* (Urbana, Ill.: NCTE ERIC, 1979), xi.
2. International Listening Association (ILA). For information on the ILA, log onto their web site at www.listen.org or contact James Pratt, ILA executive director.
3. Wolvin and Coakley, *Listening*, 13.
4. Further discussions related to these variables will be drawn from this helpful resource: Judee K. Burgoon, David B. Buller, and W. Gill Woodall, *Nonverbal Communication: The Unspoken Dialogue*, 2nd ed. (New York: McGraw-Hill, 1996).

## One: Ministry and Listening Leadership

1. Ingmar Bergman, *Private Confessions*, trans. Joan Tate (New York: Arcade, 1997), 157.
2. This was remedied in the latest revised Vision Statement of Gettysburg Lutheran Seminary, Gettysburg, Pennsylvania, which says in part: "As we listen to God' s Word in community, the Holy Spirit empowers us to lead in church and world through worship, education, service and encouragement."

3. Barbara Brown Taylor, *When God Is Silent* (Cambridge: Crowley, 1998). This work contains Taylor' s 1997 Lyman Beecher Lectures on Preaching. She eloquently describes human efforts to dodge the listening required in confronting the silences in our lives.

4. See Wolvin and Coakley, *Listening,* 176–83, for documentation from several sources on the gendered nonverbal behavior that characterizes the differences between men and women during the listening process. Categories include bodily orientation, open and closed body positions, trunk lean, postural positions, gestures, head movements, facial expressions, and eye movements. For additional information see Burgoon, Buller, and Woodall, *Nonverbal Communication.*

5. Laurent A. Parks Daloz et al., *Common Fire: Leading Lives of Commitment in a Complex World* (Boston: Beacon, 1996), 3. The authors explore the meaning of commitment in the face of dissolving and shifting boundaries of all types.

6. Ibid., 30.

7. Wolvin and Coakley, *Listening,* 25.

8. Cited in Wolvin and Coakley, *Listening,* 68, from P. T. Rankin, The Measurement of the Ability to Understand Spoken Language (Ph.D. diss., University of Michigan, 1926), *Dissertation Abstracts* 12 (1952): 847.

9. Cited in Wolvin and Coakley, *Listening,* 68, from T. R. Lewis, Listening, *Review of Educational Research* 28 (April 1958): 89.

10. Cited in Wolvin and Coakley, *Listening,* 69, from D. P. Brown, Teaching Aural English, *English Journal* 39 (March 1950): 128.

11. Publication of the International Listening Association, *The Listening Post* 63 (winter 1998): 10.

12. Wolvin and Coakley, *Listening,* 69

## Two: Listening and Hearing

1. To name only a few: the extensive work of Martin Luther (though asystematic in presentation), John Calvin, Karl Barth, P. T. Forsythe, Emil Brunner, Gerhard Ebeling, Robert Jenson, and Gerhard Forde.

2. One superlative work that documents this shift is Rebecca S. Chopp, *The Power to Speak: Feminism, Language, God* (New York: Crossroad, 1991).

3. Ernest Jenni and Claus Westermann, *Theological Lexicon of the Old Testament,* vol. 3, trans. Mark E. Biddle (Peabody, Mass.: Hendrickson, 1997), 1376.

4. Ibid., 1378.

5. *The Book of the Thousand Nights and a Night,* trans. Richard Francis Burton (New York: Heritage, 1934).

6. A variety of such passages on listening include: Gen 3:8; 45:16; Exod 32:4-5; Deut 21:5-6; Lev 8:22-24; 14; 19:14; Ezek 10:5; 1 Sam 3:10b-11; 13:3b; Judg 8:22-28; Song of Sol 4:21; 7:13; Amos 5:23-24 and 8:11-12; Jer 6:10; 31:15; Pss 54:2 and 58:4-5; 94:9; Isa 37:17a; Eccles 5:1; Prov 8:32; 1 Kings 8:52.

7. J. A. Wharton, "The Shema," *Interpreter's Dictionary of the Bible* (Nashville: Abingdon, 1962), 321.

8. For the most complete grammatical description of these words, consult Gerhard Kittel, ed. *Theological Dictionary of the New Testament*, vol. 1 (Grand Rapids: Eerdmans, 1964).

According to my colleague Richard P. Carlson, associate professor of Biblical Studies, in New Testament Greek the word *akouō* is the word most used for hearing or listening. It occurs 427 times in the New Testament, 230 times in the four Gospels, and 154 times in Luke-Acts. The word itself does not distinguish between hearing and listening. Rather, the context determines whether hearing or listening is the best English concept at work. For example, in Mark 9:7 the divine voice orders, "This is my son, the beloved one. Listen to him." But from the reaction of the disciples in the story it becomes clear that they hear what Jesus says but haven't listened in terms of understanding or adopting what he says. Similarly, in Mark 4:9 (and synoptic parallels) Jesus' words could be rendered, "The one who has ears to hear, let that one hear" or "The one who has ears to listen, let that one listen."

Drawing on its Hebraic theological roots (for example, the Shema in Deut 6), the New Testament links hearing with coming to understand. To hear God's word is to understand what God is about, which in turn is the foundation for action (see especially Mark 12:28-34).

The noun derivative of *akouō* is *akoh*. Its occurrence is much less frequent—twenty-four times in the New Testament. It can mean "report" in a rather neutral sense of an oral report (see Matt 4:24; 14:1). In fact, more times than not this is how it is used. It can also refer to the act of hearing as in Gal. 3:2, 5 wherein faith and the Holy Spirit are linked with the act of hearing the proclamation of the gospel.

9. Compare Matt 17:1-8; Mark 9:2-8; and 2 Peter 1:16-18.

10. A contemporary poet, e.e. cummings, depicts the ultimate human inability to hear God in a poem entitled "here is little effie's head." The deceased, always a procrastinator in life, does not hear God's summons to rise from the dead! From *e.e. cummings: Collected Poems 1922–1938* (New York: Book of the Month Club, 1990), 58.

11. Kittel, *Theological Dictionary,* 1:219.

## Three: Pastoral Listening

1. See also listening and confessing in Matt 18:15-20.

2. President William Clinton, nationwide address, August 17, 1998.

3. *I Confess* (1953) was directed by Alfred Hitchcock; *The House of the Spirits* (1993) was directed by Billie August; and *Priest* (1994) was directed by Antonia Bird.

4. *The Rites of the Catholic Church* (New York: Pueblo, 1983), 357–465.

5. *Occasional Services* (Minneapolis: Augsburg Publishing House/ Philadelphia: Board of Publication, Lutheran Church in America, 1982), 89–98.

6. For a good review of the history of confessor and confessing penitent, see Joseph Martos, *Doors to the Sacred* (New York: Image Books, 1982), 307–64.

7. Perhaps one of the most well-honed but feared works by the general populace was the *Malleus Maleficarum,* authored by two Dominicans, Kramer (Heinrich Institoris) and Jakob Sprenger, in 1480. This famous work was the primary manual for teaching the priest to deal with exorcisms through eliciting confessions of witchcraft and other skullduggery during the era of the Inquisition. See Heinrich Institoris (alias Kramer), and Jakob Sprenger. *Malleus Maleficarum,* trans. Montague Summers (London: Pushkin, 1951).

8. "The Babylonian Captivity of the Church," *Luther's Works,* vol. 36 (Philadelphia: Muhlenberg, 1959), 81–91, and specifically 90. See also "The Holy and Blessed Sacrament of Baptism," *Luther's Works,* vol. 35 (Philadelphia: Muhlenberg, 1960), 38.

9. "The Apology to the Augsburg Confession," Art. 13.7, *The Book of Concord,* ed. Robert Kolb and Timothy J. Wengert (Minneapolis: Fortress Press, 2000).

10. Jean Calvin, *Institution Chrétienne*, vol. 4 (Editions Belles-Lettres: 1536), 88.

11. Luther's "Small Catechism" from Kolb and Wengert, eds., *Book of Concord,* 345–75.

12. Max Thurian, *Confession* (London: SCM, 1958).

13. Ibid., 111–12.

14. Jane A. Keene, *A Winter's Song* (Cleveland, Oh.: Pilgrim, 1991).

15. Rosemary Catalano Mitchell and Gail Anderson Ricciuti, *Birthings and Blessings: Liberating Services for the Inclusive Church* (New York: Cross-road, 1991), 57ff.

16. Dietrich Bonhoeffer, *Spiritual Care,* trans. Jay C. Rochelle (Minneapolis: Fortress Press, 1989), 34.

17. Seward Hiltner, *Pastoral Counseling* (Nashville: Abingdon, 1949), and *Preface to Pastoral Theology* (Nashville: Abingdon, 1958).

18. Ibid., 59.

19. Howard Clinebell, *Basic Types of Pastoral Care and Counseling* (Nashville: Abingdon, 1984).

20. Ibid., 75.

21. Ibid., 77.

22. Ibid., 76.

23. Paul W. Pruyser, *The Minister as Diagnostician: Personal Problems in Pastoral Perspective* (Philadelphia: Westminster, 1976).

24. Wayne E. Oates, *The Christian Pastor,* 3rd ed., rev. (Philadelphia: Westminster, 1982).

25. Ibid., 88–89.

26. Ibid., 240–45.

27. Ibid., 245.

28. Thomas Oden, *Pastoral Theology: Essentials of Ministry* (San Francisco: Harper & Row, 1983).

29. Charles V. Gerkin, *Prophetic Pastoral Practice: A Christian Vision of Life Together* (Nashville: Abingdon, 1991).

30. Christie Cozad Neuger, ed., *The Arts of Ministry: Feminist-Womanist Approaches* (Louisville: Westminster John Knox, 1996), 188. Emphasis added.

31. Gerard Egan, *The Skilled Helper: A Problem-Management Approach to Helping,* 5th ed. (Pacific Grove, Calif.: Brooks/Cole, 1994).

32. Ibid., 94.

33. Ibid., 106.

34. Ibid., 298.

35. Wolvin and Coakley, *Listening.* See my chapter 1 for a summary of the Wolvin-Coakley framework.

## Four: Listening and the Law

1. All three excerpts here are from the Pennsylvania State Legal Code. I am indebted to Dr. Alan Wenrich of Lower Susquehanna Synod, Evangelical Lutheran Church in America, for providing this information.

2. Richard Hammer, *Church Law and Tax Report* (Matthews, N.C.: Christian Ministry Resources, 1993).

3. See also Lindell Gumper, "Legal Issues in the Practice of Ministry," in *Psychological Studies,* 3rd ed. (West Bloomfield, Mich.: Psychological Studies and Consultation Program, 1984); Richard Hammar, *Pastor, Church and Law* (Springfield, Mo.: Gospel, 1983); Richard Causer, *Ministry and the American Legal System* (Minneapolis: Fortress Press, 1993).

4. "Ordination," *Occasional Services,* 197.

5. Evangelical Lutheran Church in America, "Vision and Expectations" (Chicago, 1990), 11–12.

6. Evangelical Lutheran Church in America, *Constitutions, Bylaws, and Continuing Resolutions* (Minneapolis: Augsburg Fortress, 1999), chap. 7, Sec. 7.45.

7. William W. Rankin, *Confidentiality and Clergy: Churches, Ethics, and the Law* (Harrisburg, Pa.: Morehouse, 1990), 132.

### Five: Listening at Heart's Edge

1. *The Rule of St. Benedict in Latin and English with Notes*, ed. Timothy Fry (Collegeville, Minn.: Liturgical Press, 1981), 157.

2. Doris Donnelly, "Listening in the Rule of St. Benedict," *Spirituality in Ecumenical Perspective*, ed. E. Glenn Hinson (Louisville: Westminster/John Knox, 1993), 33–47.

3. *The Rule*, 191.

4. Donnelly, "Listening," 42.

5. *The Rule*, 209.

6. Søren Kierkegaard, *Purity of Heart Is to Will One Thing*, trans. Douglas V. Steere (New York: Harper & Row, 1956).

7. Ibid., 177ff.

8. Ibid., 179.

9. Ibid., 180.

10. Douglas V. Steere, *On Listening to Another* (New York: Harper, 1955).

11. Wolvin and Coakley, *Listening*, 156.

12. *Webster's Seventh New Collegiate Dictionary* (Springfield, Mass.: Merriam, 1967), 237.

13. Rodney J. Hunter, ed., *Dictionary of Pastoral Theology and Counseling* (Nashville: Abingdon, 1978), 287.

14. Norma S. Wood in her installation address as Dean of the Seminary, September 8, 1998, Lutheran Theological Seminary, Gettysburg, Pa.

15. Susan Karen Hedahl, "'The Pure Word of God': The Americanization of Lutheran Homiletic Invention Theory, 1893–1922" (Ph.D. diss., Graduate Theological Union, 1988), 75.

16. An example is the Certificate in the Art of Spiritual Direction Program operated by San Francisco Theological Seminary and directed by ecumenical personnel. After an initial three-summer trial period, a certificate program is now offered by Gettysburg Lutheran Theological Seminary.

17. Some of these in use in congregational life are *The Upper Room*, reading a Bible verse from an Advent calendar, reading the lectionary inserts found in church bulletins, listening to a taped version of the pastor's sermon. It is worth the exploration of an education committee and the minister to see exactly which resources are forming the spiritual lives of

parishioners, particularly with the cross-section of nondenominational materials available today.

18. Pastor Bob Yankovitz.

## Six: Corporate Godward Listening

1. Material taken from Judee K. Burgoon, David B. Buller, and W. Gill Woodall, *Nonverbal Communication: The Unspoken Dialogue,* 2nd ed. (New York: McGraw-Hill, 1996).

2. Ibid., 33.

3. Ibid., 70.

4. Ibid., 213.

5. Ibid., 122.

6. Some deep feelings that operate at many conscious and subliminal levels are attached to this act of reconciliation. Erma Bombeck in the *Minneapolis Tribune* (1981) compared exchanging the peace to going on a "religious blind date." For more historical information on the evolution of this biblical custom, see Nicolas James Perella, *The Kiss: Sacred and Profane* (Berkeley: Univ. of California Press, 1969).

7. Two major publications on the issue of haptics and its related dimensions in ministry are Marie M. Fortune, *Is Nothing Sacred? When Sex Invades the Pastoral Relationship* (San Francisco: Harper & Row, 1989), and Peter M. Rutter, *Sex in the Forbidden Zone: When Men in Power—Therapists, Doctors, Clergy, Teachers, and Others—Betray Women's Trust.* (New York: Fawcett Crest, 1989).

8. Wolvin and Coakley, *Listening,* 89.

9. Wolvin and Coakley, *Listening,* quoting M. J. Smith, "Cognitive Schemata and Persuasive Communication: Toward a Contingency Rules Theory," in *Communication Yearbook 6,* ed. M. Burgoon (Beverly Hills, Calif.: Sage, 1982), 320–62.

10. Steven Cushing, "Air Cal Three Thirty Six, Go Around Three Thirty Six, Go Around: Linguistic Repetition in Air-Ground Communications," *Repetition in Discourse Theory: Interdisciplinary Perspectives,* vol. 2, ed. Barbara Johnstone (Norwood, N.J.: Ablex, 1994), 55.

11. Kellogg's Frosted Flakes commercial.

12. Thomas G. Long, *The Witness of Preaching* (Louisville: Westminster/John Knox, 1989), 132.

13. Phillips Brooks, *Lectures on Preaching* (London: H. R. Allenson, n.d.), 5.

14. See John McClure *The Roundtable Pulpit: Where Leadership and Preaching Meet* (Nashville: Abingdon, 1995). The book is a much-needed look at the dialogic nature of the sermon but says nothing about the role listening plays in the process.

15. *On Christian Doctrine*, trans. D. W. Robertson (Indianapolis: Bobbs-Merrill, 1958), 142. Emphasis added.

16. Martin Luther, *Luther's Works*, vol. 22 (St. Louis: Concordia, 1967), 400–401. See also WA 47 120:10–35.

17. Fred B. Craddock, *Overhearing the Gospel: Preaching and Teaching the Faith to Persons Who Have Heard It All Before* (Nashville: Abingdon, 1978).

18. Ibid., 116–18.

19. Ronald J. Allen, "Modes of Discourse for the Sermon in the Postmodern World," *Theology for Preaching; Authority, Truth, and Knowledge of God in a Postmodern Ethos*, ed. Ronald J. Allen, Barbara Shires Blaisdell, and Scott Black Johnston (Nashville; Abingdon, 1997), 161–86.

## Seven: "Where Two or Three Are Gathered"

1. For additional information, see Eric M. Eisenberg and H. L. Goodall Jr., *Organizational Communication: Balancing Creativity and Constraint* (New York: St. Martin's, 1993).

2. For example, in the Evangelical Lutheran Church in America's parish constitution, the following rule applies: "C10.07. Robert's Rules of Order, latest edition, shall govern parliamentary procedure of all meetings of this congregation." ELCA, *Constitutions, Bylaws, and Continuing Resolutions*, 191.

3. Eisenberg and Goodall, *Organizational Communication*, 255.

4. Judee K. Burgoon, David B. Buller, and W. Gill Woodall, *Nonverbal Communication: The Unspoken Dialogue*, 2nd ed. (New York: McGraw-Hill, 1996), 345.

5. Ibid., 347–48.

6. Ibid., 348–49.

7. Ibid., 352.

8. Ibid.

9. See Robin Patric Clair, *Organizing Silence: A World of Possibilities* (Albany, N.Y.: State Univ. of New York Press, 1998), 352. The research and bibliography in this field are immense, long-standing, and fascinating.

10. Stephen Ministries, 2045 Innerbelt Business Center Drive, St. Louis, MO 63114–5765 (www.stephenministries.org).

11. See chap. 9 for information related to this course.

12. Pastor Karen Minnich-Sadler.

13. Parker J. Palmer, "The Clearness Committee: A Way of Discernment," *Weavings* (July–August, 1988): 37.

14. Ibid., 38.

15. Ibid.

16. Ibid.

17. Ibid.

18. Ibid., 38–39, italics Palmer's.

19. Ibid., 39.

20. Ibid.

21. Ibid., italics Palmer's.

22. Ibid., 40.

23. Ibid., 40.

## Eight: Listening in Community

1. Wolvin and Coakley, *Listening,* 262.

2. Hunter, *Dictionary of Pastoral Care and Counseling,* 371–72, 654.

3. The reader is encouraged to consult works on any of these specific therapeutic listening responses in the fields of organizational communication and management, psychology, communication, pastoral counseling, sociology, and physiology.

4. Wolvin and Coakley, *Listening,* 269.

5. I am grateful to Norma Schweitzer Wood, dean of our seminary and a licensed psychologist and professional counselor, for this definition.

6. Egan, *The Skilled Helper,* 94–104.

7. Ibid., 100–104.

8. Pastors William L. F. Gries and Beth Bergeron Folkemer.

9. Jorg R. Bergmann, *Discreet Indiscretions: The Social Organization of Gossip,* trans. John Bednarz Jr. with Eva Kafka Barron (New York: Aldine de Gruyter, 1993), x.

10. Ibid., 49–55.

11. Ibid., 54.

12. Ibid., 66–67.

13. Ibid., 68.

14. Ibid.

15. Ibid., 70.

16. Ibid.,vi.

17. Robert L. Montgomery, *Listening Made Easy: How to Improve Listening on the Job, at Home, and in the Community* (New York: AMACOM, 1981), 35.

18. Currently the Evangelical Lutheran Church in America is considering a proposal, now in draft form, entitled "Congregation Child Protection Policy." It details law, hiring procedures for adults, and behavioral patterns between adults and children in the parish setting.

19. See chap. 3.

20. Lecture at Gettysburg College, September 14, 1998.

21. From the brochure, "The Holocaust and Modern Memory," published for the Senior Scholars' Seminar (autumn 1998), Gettysburg College, Gettysburg, Pa.

## Nine: A Theology of Listening:

1. Consult the extensive bibliography in Gemma Corradi Fiumara, *The Other Side of Language: A Philosophy of Listening* (New York: Routledge, 1990).

2. Ibid., 3.

3. Ibid., 11.

4. Ibid., 25.

5. Ibid., chap. 6.

6. Ibid., 89.

7. See chap. 6 in Theodore Reik, *Listening with The Third Ear* (New York: Farrar, Straus, 1949), 144.

8. Taylor, *When God Is Silent,* 80.

9. *Androgogy* is an educational term that deserves our increasing attention. It refers to the instruction of adults.

10. Main offices are located in St. Louis, Mo.

11. See appendix B for one pastor's monthly newsletter invitation to his people regarding listening skills and listening to a sermon.

# Bibliography

## Books

Allen, Ronald J., Barbara Shires Blaisdell, and Scott Black Johnson, eds. *Theology for Preaching: Authority, Truth and Knowledge of God in a Postmodern Ethos.* Nashville: Abingdon, 1997.

Ashbrook, James B. *Minding the Soul: Pastoral Counseling as Remembering.* Minneapolis: Fortress Press, 1996.

Augustine, *On Christian Doctrine.* Trans. D. W. Robertson. Indianapolis: Bobbs-Merrill, 1958.

Baird, John E. *Conducting Church Meetings.* Nashville: Abingdon, 1991.

Banville, Thomas G. *How to Listen—How to Be Heard.* Chicago: Nelson-Hall, 1978.

Bergman, Ingmar. *Private Confessions.* Translated by Joan Tate. New York: Arcade, 1997.

Bergmann, Jorg R. *Discreet Indiscretions: The Social Organization of Gossip.* Translated by John Bednarz Jr., with Eva Kafka Barron. New York: Aldine De Gruyter, 1993.

Bonhoeffer, Dietrich. *Spiritual Care.* Translated by Jay C. Rochelle. Minneapolis: Fortress Press, 1989.

*The Book of the Thousand and One Nights and a Night.* Translated by Richard Francis Burton. New York: Heritage, 1934.

Brooks, Phillips. *Lectures on Preaching.* London: H. R. Allenson, n.d.

Burgoon, Judee K., David B. Buller, W. Gill Woodall. *Nonverbal Communication: The Unspoken Dialogue.* 2nd ed. New York: McGraw-Hill, 1996.

Caldwell, Taylor. *The Listener.* New York: Doubleday, 1960.

Calvin, Jean. *Institution Chrétienne.* Vol. 4 of Editions Belles-Lettres, 1536.

Causer, Richard. *Ministry and the American Legal System.* Minneapolis: Fortress Press, 1993.

Chopp, Rebecca S. *The Power To Speak: Feminism, Language, God.* New York: Crossroad, 1991.

*Christian Worship: A Hymnal.* St. Louis: Christian Board of Publication / Bethany Press, 1953.

Christie, Cozad Neuger, ed. *The Arts of Ministry: Feminist-Womanist Approaches.* Louisville: Westminster/John Knox, 1996.

Clair, Robin Patric. *Organizing Silence: A World of Possibilities.* Albany, N.Y.: State Univ. of New York Press, 1998.

Clinebell, Howard. *Basic Types of Pastoral Care and Counseling.* Rev. ed. Nashville: Abingdon, 1984.

Craddock, Fred. *Overhearing the Gospel: Preaching and Teaching the Faith to Persons Who Have Heard It All Before.* Nashville: Abingdon, 1978.

cummings, e.e. *Collected Poems 1922–1938.* New York: Book of the Month Club, 1990.

Daloz, Laurent A. Parks, Cheryl H. Keen, James P. Keen, Sharon Daloz Parks. *Common Fire: Leading Lives of Commitment in a Complex World.* Boston: Beacon, 1996.

Donnelly, Doris. "Listening in the Rule of St. Benedict." In *Spirituality in Ecumenical Perspective,* ed. E. Glenn Hinson, 33–47. Louisville: Westminster John Knox, 1993.

Egan, Gerard. *The Skilled Helper: A Problem-Management Approach to Helping.* 5th ed. Pacific Grove, Calif.: Brooks/Cole, 1994.

Eisenberg, Eric M., and H. L. Goodall Jr. *Organizational Communication: Balancing Creativity and Constraint.* New York: St. Martin's, 1993.

Evangelical Lutheran Church in America. *Constitution, Bylaws, and Continuing Resolutions.* Minneapolis: Augsburg Fortress, 1991.

——"Visions and Expectations." Chicago, 1990.

Fiumara, Gemma Corradi. *The Other Side of Language: A Philosophy of Listening.* Translated by Charles Lambert. London: Routledge, 1990.

Fortune, Marie M. *Is Nothing Sacred? When Sex Invades the Pastoral Relationship.* San Francisco: HarperSanFrancisco, 1989.

Fry, Timothy, ed. *The Rule of St. Benedict in Latin and English with Notes.* Collegeville, Minn.: Liturgical, 1981.

Gerkin, Charles V. *Prophetic Pastoral Practice: A Christian Vision of Life Together.* Nashville: Abingdon, 1991.

Hammar, Richard. *Pastor, Church and Law.* Springfield, Mo.: Gospel, 1983.

———. *Church Law and Tax Report.* Matthews, N.C.: Christian Ministry Resources, 1993.

Hammarskjöld, Dag. *Markings.* New York: Knopf, 1964.

Hedahl, Susan Karen. "The Pure Word of God": The Americanization of Lutheran Homiletical Invention Theory, 1893–1922. Ph.D. diss., Graduate Theological Union, 1988.

Hiltner, Seward. *Preface to Pastoral Theology.* Nashville: Abingdon, 1958.

———. *Pastoral Counseling.* Nashville: Abingdon, 1949.

Hinson, Glenn E. *Spirituality in Ecumenical Perspective.* Louisville: Westminster/John Knox, 1993.

Hunter, Rodney J. *Dictionary of Pastoral Care and Counseling.* Nashville: Abingdon, 1990.

Institoris, Heinrich (alias Kramer), and Jakob Sprenger. *Malleus Maleficarum.* Translated by Montague Summers. London: Pushkin, 1951.

*Interpreter's Dictionary of the Bible.* Nashville: Abingdon, 1962.

Jenni, Ernest, and Claus Westermann. *Theological Lexicon of the Old Testament.* Vol. 3. Translated by Mark E. Biddle. Peabody, Mass.: Hendrickson, 1997.

Johnstone, Barbara. *Repetition in Discourse: Interdisciplinary Perspectives.* Vols. 2 and 48 of *Advances in Discourse Processes.* Norwood, N.J.: Ablex, 1994.

Keene, Jane A. *A Winter's Song: A Liturgy for Women Seeking Healing from Sexual Abuse in Childhood.* Cleveland: Pilgrim, 1991.

Kierkegaard, Søren. *Purity of Heart Is to Will One Thing.* Translated by Douglas V. Steere. New York: Harper & Row, 1956.

Kittel, Gerhard, ed. *Theological Dictionary of the New Testament.* Vol. 1. Grand Rapids: Eerdmans, 1964.

Koile, Earl. *Listening as a Way of Becoming.* Waco, Tex.: Regency, 1977.

Kolb, Robert, and Timothy J. Wengert, eds. *The Book of Concord.* Minneapolis: Fortress Press, 2000.

Long, Thomas G. *The Witness of Preaching.* Louisville: Westminster/John Knox, 1989.

Lundsteen, Sara W. *Listening: Its Impact on Reading and Other Language Arts.* Urbana, Ill.: NCTE ERIC, 1979.

*Luther's Works.* Vol. 36. E. Theodore Bachmann and Helmut T. Lehmann, eds. Philadelphia: Muhlenberg, 1959.

*Luther's Works.* Vol. 35. Abdel Ross Wentz and Helmut T. Lehmann, eds. Philadelphia: Muhlenberg, 1960.

*Luther's Works.* Vol. 22. Jaroslav Pelikan, ed. St. Louis, Mo.: Concordia, 1967.

Martos, Joseph. *Doors to the Sacred: A Historical Introduction to Sacraments in the Catholic Church.* New York: Image, 1982.

McClure, John. *The Roundtable Pulpit: Where Leadership and Preaching Meet.* Nashville: Abingdon, 1995.

McNeill, John T. *A History of the Cure of Souls.* New York: Harper & Brothers, 1951.

Mitchell, Rosemary Catalano, and Gail Anderson Ricciuti. *Birthings and Blessings: Liberating Worship Services for the Inclusive Church.* New York: Crossroad, 1991.

Montgomery, Robert L. *Listening Made Easy: How to Improve Listening on the Job, at Home, and in the Community.* New York: AMACON, 1981.

Moran, Frances M. *Listening: A Pastoral Style.* Alexandra, Australia: Dwyer, 1996.

Neuger, Christie Cozad, ed. *The Arts of Ministry: Feminist-Womanist Approaches.* Louisville: Westminster/John Knox, 1996.

*The New Interpreter's Bible.* Vol. 1. Nashville: Abingdon, 1994.

Nichols, Michael P. *The Lost Art of Listening.* London: Guildford, 1995.

Norris, Kathleen. *Dakota: A Spiritual Geography.* New York: Ticknor & Fields, 1993.

Oates, Wayne E. *The Christian Pastor.* 3rd ed. Philadelphia: Westminster, 1982.

*Occasional Services.* Minneapolis: Augsburg; Philadelphia: Board of Publication, Lutheran Church in America, 1982.

Oden, Thomas C. *Pastoral Theology: Essentials of Ministry.* San Francisco: Harper & Row, 1983.

Patton, John. *Pastoral Counseling: A Ministry of the Church.* Nashville: Abingdon, 1983.

Perella, Nicholas James. *The Kiss: Sacred and Profane.* Berkeley: Univ. of California Press, 1969.

Pruyser, Paul W. *The Minister as Diagnostician: Personal Problems in Pastoral Perspective.* Philadelphia: Westminster, 1976.

Rankin, William W. *Confidentiality and Clergy: Churches, Ethics and the Law.* Harrisburg, Pa.: Morehouse, 1990.

Reik, Theodor. *Listening with the Third Ear: The Inner Experience of a Psychoanalyst.* New York: Farrar, Straus, 1949.

*The Rites of the Catholic Church.* New York: Pueblo, 1983.

Robert, General H. M. *Robert's Rules of Order.* Tamarac, Fla.: Poor House, 1982.

Rutter, Peter M. *Sex in the Forbidden Zone: When Men in Power—Therapists, Doctors, Clergy, Teachers, and Others—Betray Women's Trust.* New York: Fawcett Crest, 1989.

Savage, John S. *Listening and Caring Skills in Ministry: A Guide for Pastors, Counselors, and Small Groups.* Nashville: Abingdon, 1996.

Steere, Douglas V. *On Listening to Another.* New York: Harper and Brothers, 1955.

Steere, Douglas V., ed. *Quaker Spirituality: Selected Writings.* New York: Paulist, 1984.

Taylor, Barbara Brown. *When God Is Silent.* Cambridge: Cowley, 1998.

Taylor, Charles W. *The Skilled Pastor: Counseling as the Practice of Theology.* Minneapolis: Fortress Press, 1991.

Thurian, Max. *Confession.* London: SCM, 1958.

Tournier, Paul. *A Listening Ear: Reflections on Christian Caring.* Translated by Edwin Hudson. Minneapolis: Augsburg, 1984.

Wolvin, Andrew, and Carolyn Gwynn Coakley. *Listening.* 5th ed. Chicago: Brown and Benchmark, 1996.

Wolvin, Andrew, and Carolyn Gwynn Coakley, eds. *Perspectives on Listening.* Norwood, N.J.: Ablex, 1993.

## Articles

Erland, Walter. "The Emphasis on Hearing/Listening in the New Testament Accounts." Paper presented at a meeting of the International Listening Association, March 1991.

Palmer, Parker. "The Clearness Committee: A Way of Discernment." *Weavings* (July–August, 1988): 38–40.

Wood, Norma Schweitzer. Installation address as dean of the seminary, September 9, 1998. Chapel of the Abiding Presence, Gettysburg Lutheran Theological Seminary, Gettysburg, Pa. *Seminary Ridge Review* 1:1.

Zink-Sawyer, Beverly. "'The Word Purely Preached and Heard': The Listeners and the Homiletical Endeavor." *Interpretation* 51:4 (1997): 342–57.

## Journals

*International Journal of Listening.*

*The Listening Post.* Publication of the International Listening Association.

## Internet Resource

International Listening Association: www.listen.org